Halloween History

Halloween's Traditions and Untold Horror Stories

(The Truth About the Origination of Our American Halloween)

Jerrell Kuhlman

Published By **Bengion Cosalas**

Jerrell Kuhlman

Halloween History: Halloween's Traditions and Untold Horror Stories (The Truth About the Origination of Our American Halloween)

ISBN 978-1-77485-917-9

No part of this guidebook shall be reproduced in any form without permission in writing from the publisher except in the case of brief quotations embodied in critical articles or reviews.

Legal & Disclaimer

The information contained in this ebook is not designed to replace or take the place of any form of medicine or professional medical advice. The information in this ebook has been provided for educational & entertainment purposes only.

The information contained in this book has been compiled from sources deemed reliable, and it is accurate to the best of the Author's knowledge; however, the Author cannot guarantee its accuracy and validity and cannot be held liable for any errors or omissions. Changes are periodically made to this book. You must consult your doctor or get professional medical advice before using any of the suggested remedies, techniques, or information in this book.

TABLE OF CONTENTS

Introduction

In every any society around the globe there is always an occasion to celebrate. Celebrations can take various forms, different rituals and meanings of which one is more significant than one celebration or. The majority of societies enjoy a meal or celebration because their forefathers or, in certain instances, their ancestors, were doing the same even as they were growing to be. These traditions were passed through word of mouth or in constant practice, to serve as an example to the new generation. Most of the festivals have occurred and remained in societies. People from other societies and all over the globe know about the celebrations or are fascinated to the point of attending and participating in the celebration spirit.

Different types of feasts mean different things for different people. the majority of people feel pleasure, joy, learning and relaxation in celebrations, especially in regions that have them as essential parts of their old or modern-day cultures. In general, celebrations consist of all acts, rituals or ways of expressing gratitude, appreciation, gratitude or satisfaction over a specific religious, spiritual or social celebration, generally in a spirit of reverence or remembrance. Celebrations can also be any formal or social gathering that records the attendance of those who share the same beliefs and the same perspective on the occasion being observed and guests, typically for entertainment, fun catching , and socializing in certain cases. It could be a party or fun-fair, or just a basic gathering.

They prove the fact that festivals are celebrated with a sense of importance and esteem everywhere they are observed regardless of the way they are carried out. Many of these festival-like festivals have been a hit all over the world and allowed people to enjoy themselves eating, drinking and show off different costumes and connect with new and similarly involved people. Many of them have been ranked at the top of the list of festivals across the globe because of their popularity, the huge crowd as well as the significant impact they have on the celebrations. Certain commemorations bear an inscription in the halls of the past, and others are merely an ordinary thing such as birthdays, anniversaries, and house warming celebrations.

The ones with a lot of and fascinating history are often the most desired as well as ranked and observed among other. The past has revealed to us by way of vivid images that these rites and celebrations belong to four different faith-based sects, such as Secularism, Paganism, Islam as well as Christianity. The many feasts mentioned and their hosts have been proven to be in one way or the other, tied to at least one from these four sects. Sometimes, if they are not, then the celebrations are observed with great respect and adhering to the protocols of these sects. They reflect on the dates they beginning, the attire that is required to wear as well as the food that must be cooked, shared , and consumed, the dances to be performed as well as the prayers that are to be offered as well as rituals that must be observed and a numerous other rules as well as the type of notes that the celebrations are to be closed. There are Christmas that is actually derived from the Germanicand Norse Yule however it is usually connected to the Christians. Thanksgiving is observed by Americans both religious and secular and also New Year as celebrated secularly and in various varieties that are part of Zodiac as well as other Astrological Systems, at various dates. However, as far when it comes to the pagan religion and its origins there is the Celtic Halloween.

The Celtic group is a part of Indo-European settlements. They are also considered to be the people of ancient times in Western Europe called the Celtae by their neighbors, the Romans. After Caesar defeated many of the Celtic communities, Roman propaganda attempted mixing the divinity of the Druidic religion with the completely diverse pagan cultic beliefs regarding Roman divinities and gods. In the Post Gaelic War Celts were thought to have lived as pagans, with no reverence or belief in the concept of "The Divine" performing a shaky rituals that showed them to be quite different from their predecessors. The church's first father Tertullian stated during the 2nd century about how quickly Christianity was spreading across the Celtic areas, a distance from the reach of Pagan Romans. When it comes to details about the pre-Saint Patrick Celtic Christianity, many items are kept hidden by vows, and many were hidden in the history. Some believe they believe that the beliefs of Druidry continued to be taught in Celtic Christianity, but many Roman Scholars denied this declaring Christianity was not widely spread prior to the time Saint Patrick was born.

The past has shown that, as recently as Halloween is, it also is a tradition that dates back into early Celtic people. In the end, it is the Oxford Dictionary defines "Halloween" as the day before All Hallow's Day which is celebrated on the 31st of October. It is most often in countries such as that of United Kingdom, Ireland, United States of America and Canada which is usually marked by children who knock on doors with costumes that are deemed to be scary or scary costumes, demanding candy, and posing as dangers. Halloween is considered to be a thrilling and scary in the countries where it is celebrating. Before it gets all spooky, and bone-shaky due to the gory details of Halloween, it is important to note the way it is interwoven with the traditional Samhain festival.

Samhain According to research is according to research, a Gaelic festival that marks the end of the harvest season as well as the start of winter, the "Darker half" during the entire year. It is typically celebrated from the 31st of October through 1st November, which is when the Celtic day starts and ends at sunset. Additionally, it states that it falls around halfway between the autumn the equinox, and the winter solstice. In this definition, it is noted that Gaelic as well as Celtic are both mentioned, it is clear that there's a link that is drawn from Samhain and the Halloween festival. The Gaelic and Celtic, to connect to make it even more clear, are people who are related to Celtic and the Celtic inhabitants of Scotland, Ireland and the Manx. This is proof it is true that Celtic as well as the Celtic Gaelic tribes are closely related to each other, as Samhain is and Halloween. It is believed that Samhain festival was celebrated widely throughout Ireland and Scotland and in the Isle of Man. It is also known that similar celebrations were observed during that time of year in other Celtic regions, including the Halloween celebration could include and preemptive.

It is believed that the Celts are known for celebrating four major holidays throughout the year. The origins of Halloween is traced to the Celt's fall festival , which was observed on the first day of the month of the 11th named"the Samhain month Irish and to be November English. The festival is called by other names in many different Celtic countries, but there is usually a certain resemblance that is apparent even when translated.

It is believed that the Samhain festival is believed to be of Celtic pagan roots. And there is evidence that suggests that it's been a significant event since the time of the early ages. There was a strong belief system that was widely spread, known as"the Mound of Hostages. This was an ancient tomb on the Hill of Tara, and it was believed to be aligned to the Samhain sunrise. It was one of the first indications that it was the holiday time. This was noted in several sections of the oldest Irish literature, as well as a lot of other significant events in Irish mythology, that the majority of the festivities are in Celt and Gaelic start or occur with Samhain. It was the moment when cattle returned from their summer pastures, and also when animals were killed for the winter ahead. Bonfires with special lighting were lit because it was believed that a single fire served as a symbol of protection and cleansing power. Particularly, those bonfires that are lit through the flame of Tara. In a spiritual sense Samhain was viewed as the liminal period (which implies that it is related to the point of threshold or entry or the point of beginning) which signified when the boundaries between the realm for the living as well as the dead was more quickly be crossed opening both the deceased and the living, and in reverse.

It has been discovered to be the case that Roman Catholic All Saints Day as well as

Halloween are inextricably linked. To confirm the previous assertion of Samhain is linked to Halloween are connected in some way, it is essential to note of the fact that, during the Brythonic branch of the Celtic languages, Samhain was known as the 'Calends in Winter.' The Brythonic areas in Wales, Brittany, and Cornwall held festivals on the same day of October, which was similar to the one of Gaelic. The festival was known as Calan Gaeaf in Wales, Allantide in Cornwall and Kalan Goanv in Brittany. The Manx celebration was the first celebration of New Year's Eve on same date, which was October 31st. At these occasions the children cut turnips instead pumpkins and carried them around their neighborhood as they sang songs typically.

The All Saints or All Hallows Roman Catholic holy day was established in 609. It was originally celebrated on May 13th. In 835, an individual named Louis the Pious changed the date from May 13th to

November 1st during the Carolingian Empire's request of holy Father pope Gregory IV. Prior to that, there had been a number of testimonies, particularly those from Pseudo Bede, that the churches that now is now Germany along with England had already been celebrating this feast around the first of November and was believed to have been established in the early 8th century. This is why Louis the Pious was in response to these rumours and the evidence, established an official practice to celebrate the day of the feast. The significance and connection to the whole thing are revealed in James Frazer's claim that the date of November 1st was chosen due to the fact that it was the day of the Celtic festival of the dead. Be aware that All Saint Day is a celebration that honors the life and work of saints who died who were part of the Catholic catechumens and the doctrine. The belief is that Celts although they were pagan and had a profound influence over their English neighbors, who were Christians as well as the English missionaries also had influence on the Germans who were close with the Gaelic. Ronald Hutton even pointed out that the churches of the 7th/8th century in Ireland were known to celebrate All Saints Day on 20th April which suggests that the widely popular November 1st celebration was more of the product of a Germanic idea than one that was Celtic. As time passed from then the night of 31st of October was referred to as the'Eve of All Hallows', which was the night before All Saints Day. Samhain as a whole strongly affected the All Hallows' Eve celebration, and in turn, All Hallows' Eve. All three feasts evolved into the secular holiday of Halloween which is sometimes called The Celtic Halloween since it originated from the region mentioned.

A strong connection was drawn between not just Celtic Halloween and the Samhain and All Saints' day also. The way they're linked has been established. further connections will be revealed when the myths, traditions and myths are scrutinized and discussed. First, a humorous aspect of these tracings is that, as kids and adults wait for the arrival of the evening of October 31st, to join in the celebration of Halloween, very few can actually explain how the holiday was born. However, a few have traced it back to the early Celtic origins in Samhain. Samhain festival. Incredibly, these accounts state it was in Celtic Ireland some 2000 years ago, Samhain was the division of the year into the lighter half of the year of the year, which was summer, and the darker one that was winter. In addition, it is said that the Samhain caused the space between the world of this and the world of the other becoming the thinnest of its kind and allowed spirits to move through. Other events like the Samhain were recorded , of which one was the Hindu Diwali. It was also known by the name of Festival of Light, which coincided with exactly the time of Samhain. It was the

Hindu New Year was celebrated with Diwali similar to Samhain, which is this New Celtic Year. This has created quite many debates that resulted from speculations about assertions that claim that Diwali and Samhain share a commonality in their roots in antiquity. The debates continue for a long time. Similar information has been floating from festivals that seem to be similar to Samhain in both the meaning dates, meaning, and traditions However, none has been considered to be comparable to it. This is because the Samhain's history, culture as well as myths and legends are all unique. It is believed that the Celtic Halloween and the All Saints Day are the two only festivals which are in line with Samhain and are considered to be part of it, and safely.

Naturally, most Halloween practices can be traced to the early Celtic holiday for the celebration of dead. Halloween is a celebration of various mystical customs, but each has a background or at the very least a tale to explain it. Costumes such as the wearing of costumes, or wandering from door-to-door seeking sweets can be traced back through the Celtic period as well as the early centuries of the Christian period, when it was believed that the spirits from the deceased were wandering around and about, as were fairies as well as witches and demons. Food and drinks were put out to appease the spirits. As time passed the people began dressing as the gruesome creatures and doing antics for drinks and food. This is known as "mumming," literally translating to dressing up or appearing as Mummies. This is where the tradition of trick-or-treating developed. Even today the ghosts, witches, and skeletons that are dead have been some of the most popular costumes. Halloween has also retained some aspects that are reminiscent of the traditional harvest festival of Samhain, like the custom of bobbing apples for bobbing and carving vegetables, in addition to the nuts, fruits, and spices that are that are associated with the holiday. Nowadays, Halloween is again a holiday for adults or masquerade event, similar to Mardi Gras. Women and men with every costume imaginable are walking the streets of major American cities, and gliding through glowingly carved, candlelit Jack O'lanterns and reliving traditions that have a long lineage. The masked clowns challenge, make fun of, and sooth the terrifying forces of night and soul and of the realm which is now ours during this night of inverted roles, reversible possibilities roles and transcendence. While doing this they affirm death and its role in the world in a thrilling celebration of a magical and holy night.

Chapter 1: Celtic Samhain Ancient Traditions

We agree with the idea that Celtic Halloween and the Gaelic Samhain are of a common ancestor It is appropriate to celebrate the customs and customs that are associated with them all. The customs associated with Celtic Halloween have been practices that were practiced since the time of memorial until the current time.

As mentioned earlier one of the main customs associated with the celebration includes the burning of bonfires, which were believed to have cleansing and protective power. People would perform ceremonies around the bonfires, believing that they draw power from it to create a positive impact on the world of living. The veil that separated this world and realm of the spirit was believed to have been lifted fairies and spirits were able to enter this world and communicate to the living. One of them was Aos Si, which was being that had to be blessed to ensure that people as well as their livestock were taken care of and able to survive the coming winter. To woo this spirit and other beings who sought protection, offerings such as food and drinks were placed out to them. Additionally, the spirits of the dead were believed to visit their homes to seeking of hospitality duration of the feast was on. While taking the wandering relatives into account, many there were many feats performed, and during the meal it was the custom to call the names of deceased relatives were invited to be invited to join the feast. There was a space set to them at the table in the eating area to relax and share meals with their living relatives. There was a lot of singing and dancing during the festivities as well. It was about people in specific costumes, and walking from door-to-door and singing verses to entertain the crowd and then offer them food to eat. Some believed that costumes were an attempt to conceal them from the Aos Si. Others believed that it was a method to mimic the ritual. It was a common feature in nearly all the old rituals There were divinations and games that typically involved using nuts as well as apples.

It is believed that the Irish mythology also included some rituals that were recorded, as they was related to the traditional version of the Celtic Halloween. The mythology was originally an oral tradition, but it was recorded by a few Christian monks back in the middle of the ages. The Irish mythology reveals a lot about the Samhain and tells us that it was among the four celebrations that took place on a regular basis. A tale from the 10th century titled "The The Wooing of the Emer" mentions that the Samhain was one of the first four celebrations that took place during the quarter day. In a different Irish legend, it was claimed that the event that was referred to as"the Ulaid at Samhain was held for a week, while Samhain actual celebration was celebrated for three days before and the following three days. The people of the common man would gather in a spot known as"the plain" of Muirthemni in which they could observe various games and gatherings. The feasting would be followed shortly. The story is not deficient in stating that the main feature of the meal was alcohol. The celebration did not end without a flood of alcoholic beverages that caused the majority of the attendees in drunkenness. Therefore, the festivities were considered to be the best method to experience a high spirit and let loose the mind completely. Samhain, in this sense was associated with drinking, and a lot of metaphorical assertions today refer to it as an "high" idea. In the same way, it was believed that the line between the realm of the living and the rest of the world was lifted However, while Bealtaine was predominantly an Irish celebration of summer, Samhain was in essence a celebration to commemorate the dead, and was nothing more. "The Boyhood

Deeds" of Fionn states it was believed that the sidhe (fairy mounds or portals into portals to the Otherworld) "were constantly open during Samhain". In that story, Aillen emerges from the alternate world each year and fires Tara as he lulls everyone into sleep. On one Samhain, youthful Fionn Mac Cumhaill manages to remain awake and kills Aillen and is made head of the fianna.

The night also marked also the Great Sabbat as it concerned witches. The night that was, and now is known as Hallowmas it was believed that the various covens of witches would gather to celebrate a feast. They would gather in large numbers to cast spells, create predictions and celebrate the celebration of Samhain. As folklore tells us that, in the past, witches would ride on eggshells and broomsticks, and use them to aid in their flight through the air. There were instances where they flew on ravens, black cats and horses during their extravagant Hallowmas Ride.

In fear of becoming an unfortunate victim or collateral damage the individuals would stay inside their homes in fear of stepping out out in the out in the open. The majority of the observations were made through windows. A few of the reports of these rural folk claimed there was a Queen Witches is believed to be the Irish Morrigan who was sometimes referred to as Morgan le Fay. In other mythologies the Blue Faced Hag of Winter was and sometimes known as the Calleach was the sole head on the night before the Hallowmas Ride. The story was told in this context by one of Clan Donald, Kenneth Wiepert. The story was about the clan's version of witches. The story was told that the MacDonald's from Glen Coe had their own witch and she was the type of witch known as a Water Witch. She was renowned for her beautiful and soft skin, which was matched with her hair that was red. According to the legend, she was often seen in the most white of robs, and an black cape that covered the cape behind. The cap is believed to have been black as the night itself and certain accounts claim it. Name of this fair, white skinned and red-haired Water Witch was Sidiethe. She would often stand and singing along the shores of Loche Linhe, near Glen Coe. Her songs were thought to be beautiful and her voice was powerful enough to slice your heart. The majority of the time she was crying and singing simultaneously, evidently waiting for the onset at the Samhain festival, when she would gather with her colleagues and use their talents. Just prior to a massacre that was committed within Glen Coe in 1962, she was seen washing her clothes in the River Ford while she wept and in some stories, sang along. The story goes that this would always happen prior to the tragic death of a certain household. There are many accounts that have told her story in various ways. In more ways than one have said that she washed clothes and weeping during that night, which is Samhain. Numerous sightings of the witch's ghost can be traced to the 1100s. Many of the tales from this time period claimed that she was also referred to by the name of White Witch of Glen Coe. The ghost is often associated with Hallowmas. Numerous scholars have disproved this as a vivid illustration of the waiting time of witches in the night of Samhain to reunite with their departed friends and with those who live to perform spells, and fly through the glitz of celebration.

There are other Irish stories suggest that offerings, libations, or sacrifices were offered during Samhain. Samhain festival. It was said as part of the legend that each Samhain celebration, the inhabitants of a village called the Nemeds had to hand at least two-thirds of their children along with their corn and milk to the monsters known as the Fomorians. The word "fomorian" means "monstrous". Fomorian is the semi-divine race thought to have lived in Ireland during the time of the ancients. There are those who believe they were creatures, not human beings. Their strength and presence increased as the veil between the two worlds was lifted and the Irish were required to do the will of God to prevent the wrath of God to be hurled at them. The Fomorians were thought to be symbol of the destructive and destructive force of nature. These were all powerful symbolisms for chaos and doom, anarchy, peril, darkness as well as death, blight, and drought, to name a few. The offering of two-thirds of the inhabitants of Nemed was a symbol of the ritual sacrifice typically made at the start of winter, when the power that bring darkness as well as blight are on the ascendance. In the Annals of the Four Masters was a different story that claimed that Samhain in the early days of Ireland was connected to an Idol or god that was known as Crom Cruach. The story's specifics state that the child's firstborn was required to be sacrificed to the idol made of stone by the god to be appoint him. This was the aid was granted to King

Tigernmas from Ireland and his three-fourths of sons were all stricken as they prayed to the god on the festivals of Samhain. The legends of the Kings Diarmait mac Cerbaill and Muirchertach mac Ercae both suffer a triple death during Samhain, which includes burning, wounds and drowning, that they are warned about. In the legend of Togail Da Derga Bruidne "The Destruction of Da Derga's Hostel", King Conaire Mor too fell to his death on Samhain following the breaking of the geasa (prohibitions or taboos). The king was warned about his imminent death by three horsemen who were undead who were believed to be messengers for Donn god of dead. Many scholars suggest that these stories are a reference to the sacrifice of a human being, and suggest that a number of older Irish ancient bodies appear to be kings who were ritually killed by some at the time of Samhain.

Another tradition associated with Samhain that F. Marian McNeill said was that the flames at the Samhain festival were lit using the traditional force-fire way, but McNeill later mentioned that the tradition was shattered. Certain types of wood were used, however, further evidence of the aftermath revealed that a range of flammable materials were used to keep the fire going. This practice in a way suggests that fires could be a form of sympathetic or imitative magic, which means that they were akin to the sun's energy, aiding the powers that regulate growth and delaying the ones that lead to the dark winter and decay. It could also be the result of symbolic magic or a ritual which was employed to destroy all dangers and negative influences. In Moray the county located in Scotland There were rituals of children who walked around seeking fuel for the bonfires from every home within the village. It represented a villager going to his home to collect an object that was a sign of danger or backwardness in their property and then giving this item to boys to burn for consumption. As the fire was lit and the children from the community laid on the ground, one after another. They did this in the closest proximity to the flame as they could to avoid being burnt. If a young person sit on the ground next to the flame, they would sit and let the smoke engulf himwhile others around were able to go through the smoke, and then jump over him. The significance of this particular ritual is not yet known to the uninitiated. However, as it was claimed that bonfires were cleanser powers, it's simple to conclude that the heat and smoke cleansed every youth of physical and spiritual ailments and the running and jumping over other youths was a method of dissolving or removing the weaknesses into air. After the bonfire had finally be smoldering, the youngsters were still able to scatter the ashes, competing for the honor of being fortunate enough or shrewd enough to spread the largest amount. There were times when two bonfires were lit at the same time. The livestock and the people would stroll between them in a ceremony to cleanse. They would throw the bones of the carcasses of the slaughtered animals in the flames. To understand the significance of this we could look at the ancient Gaelic world of the past that used the cattle to be a sign for wealth and also as the centre of pastoral and agricultural life generally. This implies that throwing the carcasses of cattle into the flame meant that people would give of their wealth to Samhain hoping to be granted more blessings in relation to the wealth. It was in a way an investment ritual. Also, people would take in the flames of the flames and carried them back to their home. In certain parts within the Scottish empire the torches of turf or fir that was burning were scattered sun-wise over a variety of properties and fields since it was believed that they possess protection powers. In other areas where people were able to light their hearths with fires during the night of Samhain. In order to signify a type of rebirth following, each family would be solemnly lit their hearths with a fire that was a result of the bonfire shared by all. It also was a symbol of connection. Each family gathers the fire from the common bonfire. This means you are tapping into the source of renewal and cleansing. The lighting of their hearth fires by the flames was an act which brought everyone together physically and mentally, even if their bonds were broken by enmity, jealousy and disputes. This ritual brought families together with one another and facilitated peace and harmony throughout the village.

The 17th century was while burning the bonfires, Geoffrey Keating had some documents that stated that the country was home to Druids in the old Ireland and they preferred gathering around Tlaschta on the night of Samhain to ignite a sacred flame. From the furnace that was lit they would ignite every bonfire across the world and from there each home in the country would burn their hearths with a smoky glow. The process of smothering the old fire with the new fire be a tradition which symbolized the removal of evil. This is performed during New Year festivals in many nations.

Bonfires were also utilized in rituals which had to be associated with divinations. At the turn of the century there was a mention of a stone ring that were laid over the bonfire, usually with ashes in layers. The stones that were in the numbers represented those who attended the celebration. Every person would be seen running around the set of stones using an exuberant torch. The next morning, on the next day the stones were looked over, and if a missing stone was to be discovered in the group, it could be declared with the utmost of certainty that the owner of who was buried with that stone could not survive the current year. The true nature and the validity of the claims relating to the ritual is still unproven. There is no way to prove the truth that the claims were accurate. But , as far as the legends surrounding bonfires are concerned they all prove that the Samhain festival couldn't be observed and ended without the burning of a bonfire as well as the sharing of them in the form of fires that were part of families to honor and symbolise more than is apparent to the naked eye.

As previously mentioned that apples and nuts were the primary ingredients in these Samhain ceremonies. The bonfire-lit rituals were meant to include divination symbolism as it related to the people who were gathering, particularly in relation to marriage and death. Hazelnuts and apples were used to divinate during ceremony and game. The mythology associated with the Celts the apple was believed to have an extremely strong connection with issues that were associated with the world beyond, and specifically immortality. The belief was that eating the apple believed to be divine was a means of attaining immortality. However the hazelnuts were believed to be a symbol of divine wisdom, making folk believe they could miraculously learn to discern the truth after eating the fruit that had gone through the divinations during the time of the festival. A very popular games played during the celebrations was bobbing apples. A different game that is not named was the hanging of a tiny wooden rod hanging from the ceiling, at head's level and a candle lit on one side as well as an apple hanging on the other. The rod turned around in a tense manner, causing the candle as well as the apple to move away between the two ends. The arrangement would then spread and people would trying to grab the apple with their teeth . apples were sliced into one long strip and the resulting peels were dropped over the shoulder and tossed towards the back. The resulting form of the peels being tossed around was thought to be the initial letter of the peeler's spouse's name. The hazelnuts were utilized in different ways. Two of them would be cooked in front of a fire most likely the bonfire and the other one was named after the person who roast them, while the other was named in honor of the individual they wanted to fight to fight. Should the two nuts leap away from the heat it could be a poor signal. If the two nuts roasted in a quiet fire and sat quietly by the fire, it could be thought to indicate that the two people that the nuts represented were an ideal match. The nuts' distancing from each other and away from the flame could be a sign of displeasure between the two sides. This divination ritual was what the majority of unmarried women and men anticipated as they used it to determine the most suitable couples for marriage and to eliminate the undesirable ones. Foretelling was done by using foods that were hidden in food items generally cakes, as they served to conceal the presence of items.

Parts of the cakes that contained items concealed within them were served to those in attendance. The future of a person was predicted by the present they got. In most cases, finding rings on the cake signified that the person was about or fortunate to be married, typically in a relatively short minutes. If one found an unmarked coin this was a sign that wealth would be available to the person in the near future. These were all meant to prepare the couples for wedding. To bolster the divine rites the salty oatmeal bannock was baked and then given to a person who was not married to take a bite of. The person would eat three bites and then go to sleep without asking anyone to consume. It was a must to remain silent and a custom otherwise the ritual could be ruined. The consumption of oatmeal by the people could induce an unusual sleep during which they'd have dreams. The dream would feature their future spouse offering the couple water for the thirst they'd endured prior to going to bed. The dreamers were told to pay attention in their dreams , so that they could spot couples' faces since they were required to meet them in reality. In other instances eggs were thrown into the water, and the shapes they made were believed to indicate what number of kids they'd be blessed with in the future.

The Wiccans observed a different version of Samhain and also had similar customs that governed the celebration. They observed this as one of the annual Sabbats of the Wheel of the Year. The majority of them that Samhain was the most significant of the Sabbats, and as a day to commemorate people who who have passed away, which often involves the offering of tributes and a tribute to their relatives, ancestors members, relatives and elders of the faith pet friends, and others loved ones who passed away to the next world. In certain rituals it was a call from individuals to visit the spirit of those who are deceased. This was considered to be an event of darkness that is balanced at the opposite side of the wheel through The spring celebration of Beltane. Beltane is a festival of light and fertility. Beltane was a celebration which was celebrated by Wiccans as a celebration of the light and fertility. The Wiccans believe that the veil could bridge the two worlds allowed them to communicate easily with their loved ones dead. However, to the Wiccans, this did not mean that the dead couldn't be reached except for Samhain. The earliest practices of Wicca have proven that they had a connection with the dead on a variety of occasions, other that the Samhain time. It was certainly feasible for the living to communicate with the dead, but it wasn't as simple as it was is for those who are dead communicate with the living. It is believed that Samhain didn't just grant them the power to connect to the otherworld and the dead, but also gave them the power to be able to connect to them at any time without having to be summoned. The dead could meet again with the ones they left behind and also the crossers of the otherworld. The dead before the time of Samhain,, were entirely at the demand of the spiritual elders ritualists, diviners, and ritualists because they were able to answer questions and the right direction to direct their attention towards. Wiccans believed in the Samhain as a time for reconciliation, reconciliation and the resolution of unfinished business. The practice of making peace with the deceased was the main goal because they were believed to possess ability to avoid evil and protect their loved ones, and bring luck to them.

A synopsis of one of these traditions is found in Sir Walter Scott's essays. Concerning the rituals associated with Samhain the festival, he wrote:

At Hallowmas Eve, ere ye taken to sleep,

Be aware of your couch's condition. be the most beautiful;

It is a sign of the cross, and then sacrifice it with bread.

Then sing to the Ave as well as the Creed.

For Hallowmas Eve, the Night Hag will be riding

All her ninefold sweep along her side

If the wind sings low or loudly

In the moonlight or in clouds.

The one who dares to take a seat in St. Swithin's chair,

As it is Night Hag wings the troubled air,

Three questions, after he says the spell,

He should ask, and she must explain.

Of course, a writer will always have something interesting to have to say. Finding the tiniest but crucial element of every single thing and making it interesting is what they do every day. They always succeed by playing with the creative human mind, while giving reliable and solid data. This is exactly the kind of thing Walter did with this piece. The content of the piece speaks for itself. Celtic Halloween celebrations had more significance for the spiritual side than those of physical and, as the history tells us every one of them represented the peoples and modernity.

Chapter 2: Myths And Legends

It was the Celtic Samhain, as said it evolved into what we now call Halloween. It was simultaneously Irish and Celtic and a lot of what we are doing today was the customs that were practiced by the Celts. Numerous stories in the form of legends and myths have been incorporated into the folklore of Halloween, also known as Celtic Halloween, and have been incorporated into the traditions that the holiday is known to all the people who take part. Based on the American Folk Life Center at the United States Library, the Celts during Samhain costumed in diverse costumes in order to confuse various spirits wandering about and to keep from being captured and lost by them to the realm of the dead.

One of the many stories about the Samhain which were told in "Tales of the Elders" provided some readers with many things to chew and absorb. It was narrated by the tale that each year, at Samhain for

23 years, a fire-breathing creature called Aillen was able to cast charms upon the inhabitants from Tara so that they could fall into sleep. When the charms were in effect it released fire from its bowels, and then burn all the court members of Tara down throughout the night. However, there an aspiring hero called Fionn MacCumhail that stood out among the other men. He was able to stay awake by putting a sharp edge of his spear in his forehead. When the fierce creature began to wreak havoc to the court in crowd of men sleeping, Finn was wake to fight it. By using the same spear, Finn cut the creature with a lance which killed the creature. It is believed that this occurred during the festival of Samhain. In recognition of this act of heroism Fionn was named the head of Fianna. Fianna. This became the basis for Fionn's Legend of Fionn.

A Irish legend is called "The Tomb of Queen Maeve at Knocknarea" that was inspired by an old poem in the area called "Tain Bo Cuialigne," had it that of a particular queen Maeve who was from Connacht. The Queen was believed to wait until Samhain to do so before beginning with the Cattle Raid of Colley. In the course of it, she's aim was to catch the prize bull from Ulster. She is determined to capture the prize to be able to match her prize alongside her husband, Aillel. However, luck was not at her side during Samhain because the young hero Cu Chulainn fought for the Ulster until the men's birth pains were gone and gave them the courage to stand up to the Queen. The Queen was killed by the hand of Cu Chulainn and the tale of her fall was rewritten as an epitaph to the tombstone of her burial.

The myths of the region that are associated with mythology, there is the tale about Nera (or "The Rathcroghan Mound at Cruachan There was a hero named Nera who was from Cruachan who passed an endurance test of bravery set out by King Ailill. The aim was to obtain the gold-hilted sword of the King that one would leave the King's palace and proceed to the Gallows. The gallows were where the man was hung and a twig was to be placed over his ankle to prevent him from being upside-down in a downwards position. The man was supposed to do everything to avoid this. Before the hero, men had tried, but failed. They quit and gave up when their spirits were harried by them. In the night of Samhain Nera completed the challenge in a gruelling manner and successfully completed the challenge. After completing the challenge of the challenge, he demanded an ice-cold cup. After being given a cup of water the eyes appeared to be opening and he was able to see the whole royal palaces of the kingdom burning down to the earth. A fairy mounds shed an additional light on the vision to the already puzzled Nera. She explained to him that what he saw was the fate of the Kingdom if not warned. It was the abrupt conclusion of the legend, though in a different version that is mentioned within Patrick Monaghan's "Encyclopedia of Celtic Mythology and Folklore,"" Nera was capture by the fairies who were gathered from the Mound and was imprisoned till the following Samhain.

The supernatural world has been associated with the celebration that is All Hallows. In the early days of Ireland fairies were one of the multitude of creatures that walked the streets during Halloween. Based on an ancient folk song called "Allison Gross" it tells a legend of the events that led to Queen Fairy saved one man from the witch's curse during the night of Halloween. The poem is as follows:

Oh Allison Gross that lives in the tower.

The most ugly witch of the North Country...

She's transformed me into an ugly creature

and guard me as I twirl in the branches of in a trees...

As it was spelled out the last night of Hallow, even

The seely court was passing,

The Queen lit her candle on the bank with a gooey vibe.

A little bit away from the tree. I'm not going to be honest...

She's changed me to my normal shape

And I'm done with tinkering about with the tree.

It is evident that the man was made into a horrible creature, and was made to feel like trees because of the witch. The poet described the witch as the most disgusting of the North County. The man was transformed into a disgusting worm and was tied to the tree. The poet went on to claim that when Hallow was over, the fairies noticed him, got off her horse, and transformed his appearance back to his human form. Fairies were believed roam in the midst of the celebration during the feast of All Hallows, which is the time of Halloween, when the knot that separated the real world to the realm of the dead was released. The fairy was given the power as well as an means to free the victim from his plight and let him go.

Chapter 3: Halloween And The Druids

It is believed that the Druids comprised known as the "wise males" in their pagan Celtic society. For those who aren't familiar or have no secrets passed down from generations there isn't much information about their existence. However there is a belief that they were the role as priests within the Celtic religion. It was one of the major festival of the fire that marked the start of winter. There was a belief that during this time the gates that separated life from death were opened or at best, not secured. The main function that priests of the Druid priests was shield their people from spirits that could cross across. Placing spirits on the ground is believed to be the genesis of the tradition of trick or treat.

The after Gaelic War variation of this notion is that souls of those who had passed away in the course of the year were held in a state of torture. They were only released and granted peace in the event that gods were pleased with offerings made during Samhain offerings. Since the barrier between Spirit World was not as strong on the day of Halloween, it was the ideal time for divination. The Druids have been believed to have been consulted to forecast everything from the harvest of next year to the marriage chances of an individual.

Many people denounce those who criticize Druids because of their "human rituals of sacrifice." There is no evidence to support this. Animals certainly were sacrificed and it is likely that this occurred in the time of the bonfires at Samhain and Halloween. The evidence of human sacrifice is not derived from Irish texts, but rather in the written works of Greeks or Romans. This is likely to be propaganda and exaggerations in order to draw attention to that "barbarian" characteristics of Celts.

In the beginning for the non-initiated it is difficult to find out anything particulars regarding the Druids. There are just a handful of texts that are dated - the Celtic mythology and religion was mostly passed down via oral tradition. Our modern-day image of the Druid is likely part of a Romantic myth. However, at Halloween of every season, we can be excused for allowing ourselves to indulge our fantasies.

The SAMHAIN Festival and Christmas (ALL SAINTS" DAY)

In English the most common title to refer to All Saints Day was All Hallows Day. (A hallow is a saint or holy individual.) The eve or vigil of the celebration, which falls on 31 October, is widely referred to by the name of All Hallows Eve, or Halloween. Despite some concerns from Christians (including certain Catholics) over the last few times regarding the "pagan sources" associated with Halloween (see Halloween, Jack Chick and Anti-Catholicism) The ceremony was observed since the beginning, long before Irish rituals that were stripped of pagan roots (just similar to how Christmas tree was stripped of similar connotations). Christmas tree has been stripped of the same connotations) and were integrated into the popular celebrations of the holiday.

In actual fact, after the Reformation in England the celebrations on Halloween as well as All Saints Day were abolished. This was not due to them being thought to be pagan however, the people were Catholic. In later times, in Puritan regions that comprised the Northeastern United States, Halloween was banned for the exact reason. However, it was not until Irish Catholic immigrants revived the custom as a means to celebrate the vigil of All Saints Day.

All Saints Day is followed by All Souls Day, November 2nd, a day on when Catholics remember all the holy Souls who have passed away and are currently in Purgatory to be purified of their sins to allow them entry into the heavens with God at Heaven.

Today, many are celebrating Halloween, though numerous sources have claimed that the tradition originated from a pagan group of people, known as the Celts. While none of the earlier Celtic Halloween customs were included in the Christian theology, a clear link has been discovered between the Christian festival and Samhain. In the introductorily mentioned passage, Celtic Halloween, Gaelic Samhain and Christian Hallow's Day were merged into the current Halloween. Despite the factual historical assertion, there are gaps and loose ends that need to be plugged and tied accordingly. If you are asking if Christian are doctrinally able to celebrate Halloween is that is not a problem, but it doesn't mean asking the question isn't required to find some answers. The Lifeway poll finds that 49 percent of the evangelical Christians across the United States participate in Halloween. A majority

(51%) of the congregation is not averse to either Halloween completely or the context "pagan aspects." It is due to the fact that many of the stories and traditions associated with Halloween Halloween give the impression that all that is associated with the celebration is a fetish and ritualistic event that is primarily associated with demonic entities like spirits, fairies and animals. This is the opinion from "some" Christians by the way. The fact that it is viewed such is a reason to believe it. Many historians have responded to these views suggested that although the Halloween celebration is very similar to the festival of Samhain during the ancient times however, that doesn't mean that it's all barbaric. The orthodox Christians along with their religious leaders claim that, as the word evolved from the time of memorials to the present there are some gruesome aspects in the celebration of Halloween were omitted which makes the holiday one-time occasion for both adults and children to enjoy themselves and enjoy celebrations of the holiday that's it. An scholar, Nicholas Rogers, wrote the book "From pagan rituals and ceremonies to Party Night" under the publication of Oxford University Press, 2002. The author states in this book "If Samhain brought to Halloween a supernatural significance and a limiting nature, it offered little in terms of rituals, except for its fire rites. Many of them were created in conjunction with ancient holy dates such as All Souls and All Saints' day". This proves that, although Halloween is a scary and frightening event yet it's closely connected to an Christian festival that takes place on the same day as well as during the time of the dame. As per Beth Allison Barr, "this indicates that the true time of Halloween does not match the popular belief that the date of November was selected to Christianize the Samhain festival.

As per Scott P. Richert, the date that is currently November 1 was established through The pope Gregory III (731-741), in the year he dedicated a chapel for all the martyrs at Saint Peter's Basilica in Rome. Gregory directed his priests to observe this Feast of All Saints annually. The celebration was initially restricted solely to the Diocese of Rome However, Gregory IV (827-844) Pope Gregory IV (827-844) extended the celebration to the entire Church and directed it to be celebrated on the 1st day of November.

There are many customs and traditions that are associated with many customs, practices and beliefs surround Feast of All Saints just as Samhain is governed by traditions the celebration. It is always about what should be done rather than how you think it should be carried out. Around the globe there are different kinds of Christians observe the celebration in many different ways. However, none of them have, as is observed, has gone off from the basic purpose of the holidaywhich is honoring and praying for those who passed away, including family and those who are not personally known.

In France and in other Francophone countries around the world, this day is known as La Toussaint. Many flowers, particularly wreaths and chrysanthemums are carried to graves by the living and laid on tombstones and graves of loved ones who have passed away and family members. The French are avid fans of flowers. They are never bored of them, and this is their way of showing their loved ones that they love them and how eagerly anticipate being reunited with their loved ones in the end. Then, at the end of the day, flowers sparkle like they're in a meadow all over the graveyards and cemeteries across the nations. The following day, the 2nd of November, it is referred to and is observed as the All Souls' Day, also known as the Jour of Morts, also known as The Day of the Dead.

It is believed that in Mexico, Guatemala, Portugal as well as in the Spanish territory, the ritual oferndeas, also known as ofrendas are offered to the dead on the day of the funeral. To celebrate this celebration during the year in Spain along with Mexico there is a stage play called "Don Juan Tenorio" is staged traditionally to add spice to the festivities and to entertain the crowd. However, these countries consistently observed the achievements of saints everywhere in a mood of sadness and yearning. They remember the acts by their dear ones during the time their lives were still alive. They display photographs of their lives in their rooms, and then pray for their souls. Portuguese children are said to be able to celebrate their birthdays independently of the adults. They observe the santorinho, bilinho or Feis of Deus custom. Children go from door to door , knocking at the door, and when they are welcomed into the open of the doors of the residents, they are presented with cake, nuts, pomegranates as well as a variety of sweets and candles. The practice is not regulated or prohibited in Portugal. It is only for children alone, while adults must purchase the sweets and keep the treats in the store, waiting for the children's knocks. There have been no costumes recorded yet in all regions of Portugal.

Hallowmas can be celebrated throughout the Philippines. Filipinos are traditionally observed as All Saints' Day . They ask their deceased relatives to restore and clean their graves, and to lay fresh flowers on the graves. Offering prayers as well as candles, flowers as well as food and even women's offerings are offered to the dead family members. Chinese Filipinos also use incense to burn and Kim. A lot of them also stay up until the evening, holding various kinds of graveyard reunions and are typically marked by games, playing music, dancing and singing to the karaoke. Food was always a an element of events.

In nations like Austria, Argentina, Bolivia, Chile, Hungary, Italy, Lebanon, Luxemburg, Malta, Peru, Puerto Rico and the state of

Louisiana The All Saints'; Day is observed by those who bring many kinds of fragrant and gorgeous flower arrangements for the tombs of all deceased relatives. In certain parts of these countries there are people who visit the graves during the cool of the evening to light candles and offer special prayers.

In the majority, if not all English spoken countries the celebration of All Saints' is traditionally observed by singing an anthem titled "For All Saints", composed and penned by Walsham How. The most popular tune for the hymn can be found in Sine Nomine by Ralph Vaughan Williams. Other popular hymns used during worship services on this day include "I Sing a Song of the Saints of God "and "Ye Watchers and Ye Holy Ones ".

Chapter 4: The Origins Of Halloween

Halloween is a popular holiday which is observed on the 31st of October. It is among the most well-known celebrations in America currently. But where did it originate from?

The roots of Halloween can be traced back to three or two distinct traditions. This first set of customs was derived from a group of warriors living on the British Isles. They were referred to as Celts and were known to celebrate the holiday of Samhain (pronounced Saw-win. It is the Gaelic word that means "November"). Samhain was celebrated in October at Halloween, which is the last day of October similar to Halloween.

Samhain was considered to be one of the most significant holidays for them because it signified the transition of summer to winter. It was believed that the Celts believed that on this day, those who died during the previous year were able to be on the Earth again.

To ward off spirits To ward off these spirits, to ward off spirits, Celts would walk along the edges of their village and offer offerings and try to encourage spirits to remain away from their houses. They also left drinks and food out for the deceased. This practice can easily be described as the early starting point of what would later be known as trick-or-treating.

In addition to the Celtic custom of Samhain The old Romans also gave the earliest origins of Halloween. The Romans were the first to celebrate a harvest festival called Pomona. The holiday was celebrated in honor of Pomona, a Roman goddess (also known as Pomona) known as Pomona, goddess of the garden and fruits.

To show gratitude to Pomona for her bounty and to show their gratitude, the Romans would spread out nuts and apples as a honor of the harvest. Even to this day, the apples are a significant celebration of the Halloween season (in particular as candy apples or apple bobbing).

Romans celebrate Pomona

As the Romans took over their way through the British Isles, the traditions of Samhain and Pomona started to merge with one another to create one festival.

A few hundred years after that of the Romans and Celts Another influence shaped the development of Halloween. The Catholic Church started to recognize the 1st of November as All Saints Day. It was a holiday that was a celebration of all Catholic saints that did not already have a day that was their own. It was also known as All Saints' Day. was also known as All Hallows Day. This is why the night prior to All Hallows' day became the All Hallows' Night, or All Hallows Eve (just as the night preceding Christmas is also known as Christmas Eve).

The old customs that included Samhain and Pomona were already in place these traditions were changed to fit the new All Hallows Eve. This was a straightforward change because the majority of Catholic countries were still adhering to the traditional customs. In the course of time when the holiday changed from one country to another The term "All Hallows' Eve changed and altered, and finally became Hallow'een, also known as Halloween.

Halloween made its way to America through some of the early settlers, who settled in Virginia. For a long time Halloween was mostly an American holiday. However the American version of Halloween received its greatest popularity during the 1890s. Through the era, Irish immigrants came to the US and brought their Halloween customs with them.

Halloween didn't really become the popular holiday that kids know and cherish until the early 1900s, however. In the early part in the early 20th Century Halloween was continuing to gain popularity. In the mid-1950s, costumes events and trick-or-treating were well on the way to becoming American customs.

The Autumnal Equinox

Every year, the 22nd of September or September 23rd is the date of an Autumnal Equinox, and December 21st or 22nd marks The Winter Solstice. What do they have to have to do with Halloween?

It is the Autumnal Equinox, which occurs around the 22nd of September, is the day on which the sun rises exactly at the eastern point of the sky, and is set exactly in its western location. The day also is "the beginning of autumn". On this day the duration of night and daylight are the same. In reality, the term "equinox" signifies "equal". However it is the Winter Solstice, which occurs on December 21st is the longest days of the calendar (fewest duration of light). It is the day that marks the beginning of winter.

Ancient cultures had celebrations in honor of these festivals. The most popular fall celebrations were Cornucopia as well as the festivals that were celebrated in Avilon, Dionysus, Harvest Tide, Mabon, Night of the Hunter, Second Harvest along with The Wine Harvest. A lot of these celebrations were held at night, with the full moon on the 22nd of September.

A variety of ancient cultures celebrated the holiday.

celebration on the full moon closest to

September 22nd.

But they did not forget that the Celts also believed in the midpoints between solstices and equinoxes. The midpoint between two quarter positions on the sun is referred to as"cross-quarter" "cross-quarter". There are four dates throughout the year that are designated as those quarters of sun. The days that mark these are Winter Solstice (fewest hours of daylight) as well as the Vernal Equinox (the first day of spring) as well as the Summer

Solstice (most hours of daylight) and the Autumnal Equinox. So there are four cross-quarters days in addition.

This Celtic festival known as Samhain (Sow-win) is the festival that celebrated the cross-quarters day that falls between Autumnal Equinox and the Winter Solstice. As time went on and the Celts were converted to Christianity and continued to celebrate the holiday during this time of year that was referred to by the name All Saints' Day or All Hallows Day. The night prior to All Hallows' day became called All Hallows Eve (eventually Halloween).

The actual halfway point between Autumnal Equinox and the Winter Solstice is November 5th or 6th, as it is celebrated in some regions however, the date of October 31st is a popular choice for a variety of reasons. It is the one most people use to celebrate this "cross-quarter" location within the calendar.

Other holidays across the quarter comprise Groundhog Day (February 2nd),

May Day (May 1st) and the largely lost Lammas Day (August 1st). Of these four holiday celebrations Halloween was the most prominent and quickly became the second most-loved day on the calendar of the present.

Trick-or-Treating

We all know that trick-or-treating is a significant aspect of Halloween's tradition. The tradition involves children going from door to door, often dressed in costumes. While their journey progresses, the kids solicit neighbors for candy or other treats. Where did this custom originate from?

The tradition of trick-or-treating began within Ireland in Ireland and England. In the Middle Ages, there was an ancient tradition called souling. It was a ritual that was a way for the poor to go from their homes to their homes in search of meals on the All Hallows Day (November 1st). The food was provided in exchange for a promise they would pray for the dead the following day All Souls Day (November 2nd).

Through the Middle Ages, the poor

took part in a custom

Known by the name of "souling".

In the early 1800s There was a culture in Scotland called Guising. Guising was a practice that saw children dress in costumes (disguises) and went door-to-door and asked for sweets. Guising was introduced across the United States in the early 1900s, when it was referred to as trick-or-treating.

The term"trick-or-treating" was first utilized in 1927. Since then the tradition of trick-or treating has steadily increased in popularity. But, it wasn't initially widely recognized. Even in the 1930s, a lot of adults were not aware of what trick-or-treating actually was and children dressed in costumes had to explain the practice.

Some weren't a big lover of trick-or-treating. In the 1930s, some adults saw the danger of children playing in a "trick" to not receive the "treat" as an extortion or a bribe. Others believed that having children visit their neighbors was as harmful as beggars. Many children even reacted to the tradition. In 1948, some boys were seen with the banner that stated "American children shouldn't beg."

In the 1950s, however it was an established American custom. Nowadays, more than 80 percent of families intend to give candy to their children during Halloween as well as 93% of kids will be participating in trick-or treating, and also taking part in other Halloween-related events.

Halloween all over the world

Many countries around the globe observe Halloween in a manner like that of the United States. However, many countries have their own customs too. Which are the most popular customs and what are the ways these holidays are celebrated?

A very fascinating celebrations that is similar with Halloween's is The Day of the Dead. This Day of the Dead is an annual holiday that honors loved ones and relatives who have died. It falls on the 1st and 2nd along with the Catholic holiday of All Saints Day and All Souls' Days.

The most important customs connected in The Day of the Dead include family gatherings, and visiting graves of relatives who died. The most famous symbol associated with the day can be seen in the form of a skull. Skulls come in a variety of shapes, including chocolate skulls, candy skulls as well as skulls made from sweet bread!

There's also a trick-or-treating custom associated in The Day of the Dead. However, instead of telling the children "trick-or-treat!" the children are asked "?me da mi Calaverita?" ("Can you give me your little skull?")

This image is from the Mexican Day of the Dead includes

various skull-related depictions.

There are many other countries that have celebrations that have themes similar to Halloween. In China it is The Festival of the Hungry Ghosts. It was believed to be the day that ghosts of ancestors who died returned to visit. In Iran an identical custom can be observed in Nowruz (New New Year's). According to the custom that those who attend the celebration are visited and greeted by their ancestral relatives during the last days of the year.

Some countries also have halloween celebrations like trick-or-treating and Halloween are often associated with various celebrations. For instance, in The Netherlands, Germany, and Austria children take part in a tradition that is similar as trick-or-treating St. Martin's Day (Nov 11th). In Sweden Halloween is a time of celebration with Easter. There's also a trick-or-treating tradition associated in Nowruz (in Iran), that sees children dressed in shrouds and request neighbors to bring treats.

The majority of European countries now have Halloween celebrations on October 31st and in a manner that most Americans will appreciate. Modern American customs and traditions are being adapted to these countries, with costumes and fun games, as well as sweets, and Halloween-themed TV shows.

The traditional Halloween Food & Games

Certain foods and games are always connected with Halloween. What are these customs and where do they originate?

One of the first food items that were associated with Halloween was soul cakes. Soul cakes were tiny round cakes that were distributed to the needy on All Hallows' Eve (November the 1st). They are often regarded as the first types of trick-or-treating. The cakes were being made and given to children in regions of England.

Another tradition of Halloween that has endured throughout the years is the Irish sweet treat called Barmbrack. Barmbrack is a type of pastry like a sweet bread and is usually made from raisins. Barmbrack is a significant element of the Irish Halloween custom.

A small item could be placed in the barrel. These objects could be peas stick, piece fabric, coin or rings. The belief was that the item that was found in the barmbrack might represent something about the person's future. For instance the cloth represented bad luck, the coin suggested that the person could become rich and the ring indicated that the person might get married in the next year.

Candy apples are a different traditional holiday treat. They are apple slices that are typically served on sticks, and then the apple is coated with an edible coating of hard candy (in other countries, they are called candy apples). An alternative similar to the apple candy is the caramel that is an apple coated in caramel instead of the candy coating.

Of course, modern American Halloween traditions are centered around candy. Candy of every kind such as candy corn and chocolate is distributed to children who trick or treat and other party guests throughout the season of celebration, but especially during the night of the 31st of October.

The most loved game or activity that is associated with Halloween can be the bobbing of apples. Bobbing for apples goes from an Ancient Roman festival of Pomona which was a time when Romans enjoyed the harvest season. Apple bobbing involves putting apple slices in an enormous basin and then plucking them out by using just the teeth.

Sometimes, the coins would be put in the apples to win prizes to those who competed. In other instances, coins could be placed in the base of the basin and kids could try to collect them as well by using their mouths.

Another game that was popular was hanging apples on strings. Participants were then asked to eat the apple with their hands tied behind backs. The most popular variant of this game had two boys on one side of an apple, and a girl on the otherside, with both competing to win the right one to devour their share from the fruit.

Children trying eating an apple suspended

From the string.

Other activities for Halloween included trying to forecast the future. A popular tradition was to cut an apple into a long strip and throw the apple's peel over your shoulders. The idea was that the fruit would fall in the form of a letter, which represented the name of your spouse to be.

A popular ancient ritual for women who were not married was sitting in the mirror in the dark of a room. In this particular instance it was believed that if one sat down and gazed at the mirror for long enough it would reveal faces of her husband.

A popular Halloween tradition that has survived the test of time includes the telling of stories about ghosts. Ghost stories are told in a way that goes back to the very first Celtic traditions related to their celebration, Samhain. It was a festival where they believed that the spirits of their deceased relatives would come back to visit the Earth.

Today among the most popular activities for Halloween is watching horror movies or other Halloween-themed TV shows. Many times, people will gather in large numbers and enjoy these films together.

The Second Half: Halloween Folklore & Legends

The Jack O Lantern

The Jack o' Lantern is among the most well-known Halloween symbols But where did this tradition originate from? What's the significance that lies behind it?

The art of carving a jack of lantern has its roots in Irish mythology. According to an ancient Irish legend that the man known as Stingy Jack. Here's the one of the aspects of this Irish story that tells the story of Stingy Jack:

Stingy Jack was an old, miserable man who was fond of playing with anyone, including his friends and family, and even his own demon. One night, Stingy Jack invited the devil to drinks with him. Naturally, as Stingy Jack wasn't "stingy" and he was stingy, he decided not payment for his drink.

Instead, he persuaded the devil that he could turn into a coin that would later be used to pay for drinks. Instead of paying for drink, Jack decided to keep the coin. He allowed the devil be back in his normal state with the caveat that he not pester Jack for a year.

A year later, Jack tricked the devil into climbing up a tree. Jack was unable to assist him climb unless he pledged never to harass him in the next 10 years. In exchange for this promise the devil also made a promise to not take Jack's soul if Jack died.

Not long after, Jack did pass away. However, God did not want to let an unsavory character like Jack into Heaven and the devil remained true to his promise and refused to let Jack to enter his realm. When Jack was turning away and the devil took pity on him and gave him a burning piece coal so that he could see through the darkness.

To be destined to walk on the Earth for eternity, Jack carved out a turnip to store his burning coal so that it could light his way. Many Irish claimed that they had seen this ghostly figure. They started calling "Jack of Lantern". In the end, this was changed to "Jack of Lantern".

It was common in Ireland to cut jack-o lanterns using hollowed out turnips or potatoes, and even beets. But the moment that Irish immigrants arrived within America in the late 1800s they discovered a different vegetable which suited the function better. The pumpkin is a native of North America and proved to be the perfect vegetable to carve and create the lanterns known as jacks of the Lanterns which are adored and revered in the present.

Children carving a jack-o lantern

during the 1800s.

Vampires

The myth about the vampire is a myth that has persisted for years. What was the reason people used to believed in such a terrifying creature? What were the mythologies related to it?

The myths of blood-sucking monsters have been around throughout recorded history, however the concept of "vampire" did not become coined until the late 1700s. The year 1734 was the first time a novel was written that used the German word "vampir" was first used in the very first instance (pronounced "wam-peer"). Although the word is German however, the majority of the popular vampire mythology originates out of the Carpathian and Balkan Mountain regions of Eastern Europe. This could include countries like Hungary, Bulgaria, and Romania.

The mythology of vampires has changed dramatically over time. The first stories about vampires described the creature as an obese corpse in purple (bloated and purple due to drinking blood too often).

A town or village will generally suspect the presence of an apocalypse if a number of strange things started happening. For instance cattle suddenly being attacked by an unknown animal or if a person from the area was missing, these may be seen as indications that a vampire was in the area.

The biggest worry of having a suspect vampire in the vicinity was the risk that he could be a threat to other human beings, which could cause the victim to turn into a vampire too. In many societies, it was believed that women of the ages of 18 and 19 were the most likely victims that vampires ate.

Different kinds of deterrents were employed to to keep vampires away. Garlic was the most popular deterrent however, it was not just the one. Crucifixes were placed on walls or doors as well as rosary beads also used. In certain regions where mustard seeds were scattered on rooftops or scattered across the ground. It was believed that a vampire couldn't traverse the mustard seeds without having to determine the number of seeds. Also, it was believed that vampires couldn't traverse on holy ground (such as the church) and they could not traverse water bodies.

Garlic was believed to be an herb

deterrent for vampires.

The villagers of the area who generally believed in this belief were unable to figure out who the suspected vampire was. This is due to the fact that when it comes to a vampire one would suspect someone who had already died. In order to identify the perpetrator, graves needed to be excavated. If a body was discovered that was not decaying enough as it ought to have, it was assumed to be the work of a vampire.

There were a variety of methods to defeat a vampire however, the most popular was to put a wooden stake in the middle. This technique is still in use and is utilized in virtually every story that is popular about vampires. In Germany the method used to stop a vampire was the removal of a body's head and placing it on the feet of the vampire suspected to be at risk.

Gypsies preferred a stainless metal spike instead of a wood one however, other cultures claimed that simply repeating the funeral ceremony would alleviate the suffering of the vampire.

The myth of the vampire really consolidated it in the latter half of the 1800s after an Irish author by the name of Bram Stoker published a book entitled Dracula. Dracula's character Dracula totally changed the perception of people about vampires and helped to create an entire mythology connected to the story. Dracula was charming and handsome He had the power of ten men and was capable of turning himself into the form of a bat.

The popularity of Dracula led to the creation of a whole category of films and books that feature vampires as central characters. The myth of the vampire remains so firmly rooted in the psyche of our society that it is likely to remain in perpetuity.

Werewolves

Many people are familiar with the mythical werewolf But what exactly is this mythology? Where did it originate from? What is the reason it is so popular?

The term "Werewolf" originates from Old English in origin. It's a combination with"wolf" and "person," Old English words for "person" and "wolf" which means that the werewolf literally an "wolf human". The word also refers to Norse term "warg" which means "outlaw". This is fitting as the character of a werewolf is believed to be a villain out of control who commits violent crimes.

Human stories of changing into animals are prevalent across the ages and can be seen in every region of the globe. There are legends of people changing into bears, lions and even dragons. It was Eastern Europe where the legends of people turning into wolves were the most popular.

For many centuries the believed in werewolves were widespread. From the 1300s to the 1500s, and until the 1800s It was believed that such creatures weren't just possible but actually existed.

How do you get to be one? In contemporary fiction, getting bit by a werewolf is the most reliable way to be a werewolf. The idea, however, did not take off in the early 20th Century. In earlier stories the only thing one needed to wear was an adornment made of the skin of a wolf.

There are other legends that claim drinking rainwater from the paw prints of wolves led to the transformation. In Italy there was a belief that if a person lay in the open on a Wednesday, or Friday and it was an eclipse this person would turn into a werewolf (this resulted in the idea that the moon's fullness triggers the transformation of a werewolf).

In the past, people were able to identify the possibility of a werewolf. Physical characteristics like the monobrow, long, bent fingernails, or lower ears were a sign of werewolves. In some societies there was a belief that the werewolf could be identified by cutting the flesh of a person. If the werewolf was present and the fur of the werewolf could be visible beneath the flesh. In different regions there was a belief that one might have hair on their tongues if they was werewolves.

Rye and mistletoe are commonly employed to deter werewolves. Rye wreaths were put up on the doors or kept inside homes to stop werewolves from getting into. The plant known as Wolfsbane was also used for its medicinal properties and believed to cure people who werewolves are suspected to be.

The mistletoe plant was used in the past to

To ward off werewolves

The ancient Middle Eastern cultures, it was believed that one could heal werewolves by smacking the head with a knives. In

Germany they believed that simply repeating the human name of the werewolf could bring them back to their original condition. In 1935, it wasn't until when the idea of killing a werewolf using silver bullets was first introduced. The first time this method was used was in a book that was published the same year and, since then, it has been popular as the only method to take on the werewolf.

The idea of believing in werewolves may seem absurd to the majority of people. However, for people who lived centuries back, it was a popular belief that was a huge help to solve the mystery of their existence.

Ghosts

Ghosts have been around for a long time as a element of Halloween's celebration. What is the reason believers believe that ghosts exist? What is the source of these beliefs? originate?

The term "ghost" originates from the Old English word, gast which was a term that meant "breath".

In folklore, mythology and mythology as well as fiction, a ghost can be described as the ghost of deceased person. The idea that ghosts of dead could take on a physical shape and communicate with living beings has been in existence for since the time people documented their lives.

According to legends ghosts have appeared to humans in various shapes, from transparent images such as mists, vapors, wispy orbs and even life-like images.

Ghosts are often linked to a specific location or object or. For instance ghosts can be haunting a place that was significant to the person during their lifetime or even have a connection with a person who they shared a connection with.

"Brown Lady" is said to haunt the "Brown Lady" is believed to be haunted by

Raynham Hall in Norfolk, England.

The belief in ghosts comes from the cultures where the ancestral (previous generations within their families) worship was an integral element of the ancient religions. It was and is, a popular belief that everyone will be able to continue their existence after death, a "afterlife."

In many of these societies the concept of ghosts was seen as a person who was not able to go through the natural transition from the world of life in the world of the dead. Maybe the person was looking for revenge on the person who committed a wrong, or were being held in the world of Earth due to actions they'd committed a wrong.

Whatever the reason for the ghost's presence, it was soon to be seen as an indication of bad luck and to be wary of. So, as time went on and ghosts were feared, it was commonplace. The idea of ghosts as something to be feared is bolstered throughout the years by how popular it is to tell ghost tales, or taking trips to attempt to meet them.

Ghosts are typically believed to be isolated entities. There are however legends that talk of multiple ghosts as well as ghost-armed forces that haunt the same location (such as the battlefield). In addition, many people imagine ghosts of humans however, there are numerous stories about ghost animals, and even ghost trains or ghost ships.

In our modern times the belief in the supernatural remains widespread. However, it's the subject of much debate , with both skeptics as well as true believers frequently fighting about their existence.

Ghosts, whether real or not, remain in the air. From books to ghost stories and films the popular culture has established the ghost as one of the most iconic characters of Halloween.

Witches

Through time there have been numerous myths and stories about witches. What are some of these myths?

Folklore about witches has been in existence for hundreds or perhaps many thousands of years. Witches have been blamed for nearly any problem you can imagine. If livestock fell sick and died, or a family member was sick or someone was hit with a sudden flurry of luck, it's generally believed that a witch could be the cause.

Through European customs witches were usually believed to be unmarried middle-aged women. But, it is important to be aware that the typical lifespan was lower than 50 years old. So, a woman of middle age is someone who is who is in her 20s, or even early 30s.

There was a belief that witches was granted her powers after signing a pact with devil. It was believed that Satan would then seal the pact by leaving a mark upon the body of the woman. It was believed by many that this was the most effective way to identify the presence of a witch. So, if a woman was suspected of being witch the body of the woman was examined to look for evidence of this mark (which may manifest in the form an enormous mole, scar or birthmark).

Also, it was believed witches was accompanied by the help of a "familiar". The familiar was believed to be a demon who would perform the witch's will for her. It was believed that the familiar could take the form of an animal, like cow or goat and, most often it was thought to be an animal of black color. The presence of animals was another way to identify a witch accused of being.

The belief was that witches travelled with

A "familiar" like the black cat.

If a witch could be recognized, there were further tests performed to "help" determine the real identity of the witch. For instance, the person was placed at the top of a cliff , and then pushed away. If she were a witch, she'd be able to fly away. If she wasn't the witch, she would be slain to an unjust death. Another test, dubbed "dunking the witch" was also used. In this instance the witch was strapped to a chair, and submerged for a long period of time. If she was alive when she was raised above water, then she was a witch. If she died in the water, then she died an honourable death.

In the 1500s in the 1500s, there was a book circulated under the name of The Malleus Maleficarum. It was basically a manual that instructed the reader on the best methods to spot witches in the future and the best way to punish those who were found.

If the woman was discovered to be witches, the most popular way to punish her was to be burned to death at the stake. This was a method for execution, which included attaching her to stakes, and then burning her.

It is estimated that between the 1400s until the 1600s More than 50 000 women were executed due to doing witchcraft. Twenty of them were executed in the famous "Witch Trials" that occurred between February 1692 until May 1693, at Salem, Massachusetts. Nineteen of them were executed, and one died in a smashed-up state.

Thankfully that hunts and execution of witches was largely eliminated in Western society, however the myth and legend of the witch persists in public mind and will continue to be a part of our lives for the decades to be.

The Third Party: Horror Literature

Frankenstein

Frankenstein's monster is among the most instantly recognized images associated with Halloween. What is the story behind the misunderstood monster originate?

In 1816, a woman of 18 known as Mary Shelley was attending a gathering. The group was engaged in deep intellectual discussions in addition to studying the old German ghost stories in front of an open fire. The host of the evening, Lord Byron, proposed an essay contest where everyone in the group was to write their own supernatural story.

The final product of Mary Shelley's work was the novel Frankenstein. The story tells about a scientist in the midst of his career Victor Frankenstein, who creates an individual by gluing together parts of bodies from different bodies before making the new creature come to life.

The story revolves around the character of Dr. Frankenstein and his efforts to destroy and track down Frankenstein's own work.

The novel first came out in 1818, at the time Mary Shelley was 21. There was a lot of criticism from critics about the novel, however it was a hit with the people who were not astonished by it and was an instant hit.

The story was released and was almost immediately made into a stage production. There are several films of the tale The most well-known is the 1931 version, Frankenstein, which stars Boris Karloff as "the monster".

Boris Karloff portrayed "the monster"

in the film from 1931, Frankenstein.

In popular culture the monster is often called Frankenstein. However, this is incorrect since the final title, Frankenstein, refers to the doctor and not to his creation. The monster does not have an official name and, in actuality in the story, it is only mentioned by phrases like monster, creature or daemon.

Despite the unflattering portrayal of him in the film,"Frankenstein's monster" as a character "Frankenstein's Monster" can actually be described as a kind creature, who is only hated by the locals due to his imposing appearance. The depiction of the "gentle monster" is consistent across all modern adaptations to the story.

Frankenstein is considered to be one among the earliest stories of the genre of science fiction and continues to influence popular culture for over 200 years. It's spawned a whole genre of horror films and stories based on the monster.

Furthermore is the Frankenstein monster is often seen on television and in comic books, as well as on shelves in toy stores and is the most popular Halloween costume of everyone of all age groups.

Dracula

Dracula is among the most popular characters in contemporary fiction, and a enduring symbol of Halloween. What is the story behind this character? Where did he originate from? How many years has he been in the game?

The Dracula character Dracula was first presented by the author of the book Dracula which was first written in 1897 and published by a business manager from Ireland known as Bram Stoker.

The novel tells the story about Jonathan Harker who travels to Transylvania on a business visit. He is assigned to help

Dracula, the mysterious and mysterious Dracula when he tries to purchase a home in London. While being at the home of Dracula, Jonathan becomes suspicious that the Count might have a connection to a vampire. He is eventually enslaved within Dracula's castle. He must find a way to escape.

In the following episode later, in London, Dracula attempts to lure Harker's lover, Mina Murray, in attempt to transform her into also a vampire. As the story unfolds, Jonathan and Mina are introduced to Abraham Van Helsing, a well-known medical doctor and scientist who's an expert in vampires. He helps the newlyweds in their quest to find and beat the count.

When it first came out in 1897, it was immediately a hit. While it was adored by the general population, the critics and reviewers were not a fan of Stoker's Gothic horror-adventure book.

Since then the tale about Dracula was told retold numerous times. There have been live theatre productions, as well as films of the tale. The most famous version of the film was 1931, a film made by Universal Films that starred Bela Lugosi as Count Dracula. Legosi's portrayal is the character that created the current image of the character Dracula.

Bela Lugosi portrayed Count Dracula

in the film of the same name, Dracula.

Since then, the demand towards Count Dracula and vampires has been growing and there have been over 200 films featuring Count Dracula playing a central role. Dracula has also been depicted on screen by a large variety of actors. Apart from adaptations for film There have also been various comic books, novels as well as video games, television shows and even animated films inspired by the character. In addition the first novel had a huge number of sales since its first publication, and remains extremely loved by readers.

Dracula was named among the "greatest film villains" by the American Film Institute and remains one of the most sought-after costumes worn by adults and children every Halloween.

The Headless Horseman

The Headless Horseman is a legendary character who, in a variety of different ways has been part of the American Halloween tradition. Where did the story begin?

It was in 1820 that American writer Washington Irving wrote a short story entitled "The The Legend of Sleepy Hollow". This story is based off of an old German folktale that included characters who was from Tarry Town named Ichabod Crane who was a lanky, boney and superstitious schoolmaster. In the tale he's competing with Bram Bones for the affections of a young lady known as Katrina Van Tassel, the sole child of a wealthy farmer.

When Ichabod departs from a party at his Van Tassel home in the autumn night, he's chased through the countryside by the headless Horseman. The Horseman is believed represent the spirit of the German Hessian soldiers who participated during the Revolutionary War and had lost his head when struck by a cannonball.

According to the legend of the region the unfortunate soldier was then forced to go to battle each night to search for his head that was missing. (In the most contemporary versions and depictions of the legend depicting the story, the Horseman is typically depicted holding the lantern of a jack-o'-lantern instead of the head of his).

After being pursued by the headless Horseman, Ichabod disappears from the town for ever and never appears ever again. Katrina is abandoned, and eventually marries Bram Bones. While the tale is up to the reader interpret the story in their own way however, it strongly suggests that the Headless Horseman is not actually a ghost in reality, but Bram Bones in disguise.

"The The Legend of Sleepy Hollow" is among the best instances of the early American fiction that is loved by many people. The tale is told told countless times, and was shown in various styles, from animated TV specials, to big-budget motion films or even stage productions.

Ichabod The Crane as well as the headless horseman

Part Four Halloween Animals:

Black Cats

Black cats are frequently linked to Halloween. They've been seen as bad luck, and thought of as harbingers to misfortune or death. What caused them to be feared and hated throughout the ages?

It's true that black cats weren't originally considered to be "unlucky". In fact, for decades, just contrary. In many societies it was believed that black cats were considered as extremely fortunate. In the case of Ancient Egyptians, black cats were believed to have a connection to their Egyptian goddess Bastet. There was a belief that Bastet could bring luck if you kept the black cat at your house.

Sailors had black cats aboard their ships as they believed that the cats were lucky and would ensure the possibility of a successful journey. There are many superstitions associated with black cats. English, Scottish, Irish and Japanese are also influenced by superstitions that believe that black cats are lucky. For instance there was a belief that a woman who owned cats of black would have many men show interest in her.

It is most likely that this belief resulted in the change in the perception of"the black cat. In in the Middle Ages, and even in the 1600s and 1500s Many single women had been accused of witchcraft. Since a lot of single women owned black cats, they were also regarded as witches. The belief was that the cats were witches' "familiars".

A familiar was believed that it was an animal that was an extension of the witch's spirit, that allowed them to perceive and hear things even when they were not (in other terms, many believed that it was an agent for the witch). Some believed that witches could transform into cats.

They became so fervent that in the 1300s, as Europe was ravaged by the bubonic disease, cats (not only those with black fur) were taken in thousands and destroyed due to the belief that they could be the source of the outbreak.

The beliefs about black cats have been tempered and evolved after in the Middle Ages. The majority of people today do not think of accusing a cat's owner of being witches, however there are those who do not think twice when they spot a black cat approaching their route. Of course when the calendar moves towards the 31st of October every year, the images and decor featuring black felines will keep dominating the scene.

Spiders

Despite their dimensions, spiders are among the most terrorized species on the planet and are often linked to the Halloween holiday. How did they come to be this way?

They are eight-legged creatures which reside on every continent, except Antarctica. There are more than 40,000 spider species that range from .015 inches all the way to 3.5 inches in length with legs that are more than 10 inches in diameter.

The majority of spiders spin webs however, there are a variety of kinds of webs. The circular pattern that people think of when they see spider webs is called the orbweb. However, many spiders weave what's called a Tangle Web (cobweb). There are also spiders that create funnel webs which resembles an elongated tunnel.

The spiders aren't known to bite however, if they do, it's generally not more harmful than the bite of a mosquito or bee stain. But there are a few cases. The brown and black recluse spiders are both believed as deadly, but will only bite if they are feeling threatened. It is also the Australian funnel-web spider is also known to produce deadly poison. The deaths of humans caused by spider bites aren't nearly as frequent as you believe. Around 100 people have died of bites by spiders over the last century.

Over the years, many different people have recognized the advantages of spiders. For instance, in countries like Cambodia and Venezuela the tarantula is eaten and considered to be delight.

Scientists are only now getting into the habit of using spiders in a variety of innovative and exciting ways too. Researchers are studying the venom of spiders to determine whether it could be utilized in medicine to treat heart issues as well as Alzheimer's diseases. Venom is also used to control pests naturally on vegetables and fruits.

The spider has been the subject of mythology and stories for centuries. Nearly every ancient society has included spiders into their myths and legends in some way. They've represented all sorts of things from patience, malice, mischief, or even the death of a person. A variety of cultures have included spiders in myths about the origins of the universe due to the ability of spiders to weave their own web.

In the modern era the legend about the spider is replaced by the fear of spiders. Spiders are feared. referred to as Arachnophobia and is among the most

107

frequently feared fears to men. It is estimated that around 50 percent females and 10 percent of males exhibit at least some symptoms of Arachnophobia.

It's probably the fear of spiders that have caused people to think of spiders as a symbol of Halloween. At a time that we tend to focus on the things that make us nervous, it is that it is only natural for spiders to have a home in the symbolism that are associated with Halloween.

Bats

In various cultures around the globe bats have always been considered to be an unfavourable light and are thought to be evil and dark. Where did this notion originate? Why are bats so closely associated with Halloween?

Bats are mammals that are that can perform continuous flight. They fly, not through flapping wings, but instead by flapping their sprawled-out fingers (like fingers) that are webbed. A thin, smooth membrane connects the digits.

Bats comprise more than 20 percent from all mammals with more than 1,240 species. They are available in a variety of sizes and shapes. The smallest ones weigh just a tiny penny, and measure only a little over an inch long with a wingspan of around six inches. While the most massive can have wingspan that can reach six feet!

Bats are mostly insectivores, meaning that they eat insects. They move around at night by using echolocation to hunt down insects on the move. They emit a sound and are able to determine the location of an insect dependent on the length of time that it can take the noise to bounce off the bug (similar similar to how submarines use sonar in the submerged).

Bats are not all omnivores. insects. Some bats eat fruit and some eat fish. The vampire bat is able to survive in the cattle industry by sucking up blood and other mammals.

Bats are nocturnal creatures in the natural world, meaning that they rest during the day , and hunt in the night. Actually, it's their nocturnal behavior that has caused the association they have with Halloween.

They've always been a symbol of darkness as they could only be observed only at nighttime. In the past, for holidays such as the Celtic festival of Samhain It was customary to set up bonfires as part of the celebrations. In the late hours of the night when the bonfires blazed on the night, thousands of bugs would become drawn to the warmth and brightness of the flame. Since bats consume insects, they could be seen flying over the bonfires too.

The link between bats and Halloween and other festivals of the autumn like Samhain has led to the introduction of bats into contemporary holiday customs. This, in conjunction with their night-time nature and the sound they make and their spooky look, allows bats to keep their status as one of the main images associated with Halloween.

Part Five Part Five: Part Five: Couple of Extras

Haunted Attractions

"Haunted Houses" or other similar attractions that are haunted have been a popular pastime during the Halloween season. How long have these attractions been operating? What is the level of popularity they?

It is not clear what year an initial Haunted House was constructed to entertain guests. The oldest of the haunted attraction was steam-powered and were built in 1915.

In the 1960s and into the early 1970s, Haunted House attractions became very popular across in the United States and were mostly used to raise money to support schools as well as other nonprofit organisations.

In the beginning, these terrifying attraction would have performers dressed in intricate costumes and masks. They would hide in the shadows and leap out at random to terrorize or shock the patrons.

As time has progressed, the haunts evolved into more complex and intricate. Modern Haunted House could include the use of lighting effects, black lights, strobes fog machines, pipes-in-sounds and other elaborate effects. Additionally, gory and intense images, as well as scenes of torture and terror are typical features in modern haunted attractions.

The phrase "Haunted House" can also be confusing. In the present haunted attractions can be located in abandoned hospitals or warehouse, basement factory or even a cornfield.

Haunted Houses are also a massive business. They are also very popular with tourists. Haunted House usually costs anywhere between $5 and $25 dollars

There are more than two thousand haunted attractions that are open each year, entertaining over 12 million terrifiedbut delighted patrons. These attractions generate billions of dollars during the time they are open, and usually leave a lot of guests anticipating the next year's visit as they come to return for more.

Phobias

Many people are afraid of something or another. What is it that makes a person frightened?

Simply simply, a phobia refers to being scared of something. It is most accurately described as an extreme, irrational and persistent fear of certain circumstances such as activities, things or even people.

Phobias are classified into three distinct groups. The three groups are social fears, Agoraphobia, and specific fears.

Social phobias are often called social Anxiety Disorder. Social phobia is defined as a constant deep, persistent, and constant anxiety about being judged by other people or possibly being judged or disgraced by one's own actions. People suffering from social phobia may be adamant to avoid social situations.

This usually is the case for large groups of individuals. Small groups of people is unlikely to create anxiety or fear. It is worth noting that someone with social anxiety isn't scared of other people however they are scared of making a embarrassing or embarrassing mistake.

Physical symptoms of social anxiety could include sweating, excessive blushing or trembling, an elevated heart rate, stammering or stuttering and nausea.

The second kind of anxiety is Agoraphobia. The term Agoraphobia refers to "fear of the marketplace". It's often thought of as the fear of situations one feels they are unable to escape from. In the context of common culture, Agoraphobia is usually known as a fear of large open spaces. One-in-five American adults -- 24 percentage of women and 17.4 percent of men -- claim they experience some anxiety about being in a crowd-filled market or open spaces.

Although a minor fear could be normal, people who develop Agoraphobia are more afraid to leave their home or go to any place they believe to be an "safe area". A few people develop severe Agoraphobia until the extent that they haven't even ever left their home in twenty years.

The third kind of phobia are the specific fears. Particular phobias are the ones that people imagine when they think of the word "phobia". This could refer to a particular fear of a particular subject for example, spiders, snakes or clowns.

To be considered a phobia the fear has to be extreme and unfounded. For instance, a lot of people are scared of snakes but their fear is not arousing. People who have a real fear could not even be in a position to see the snake, or perhaps even take a picture of the snake.

The most prominent symptom of anxiety is avoidance. The person will try to avoid the subject of their fear at all cost. For instance, someone who is afraid of snakes would stay clear of situations where there may even be a chance that they might come into contact with the snake (like going camping).

Phobias are among the most commonly encountered psychological disorders. And According to National Institute of Mental Health As high as one out of 10 Americans are suffering from any form of fear.

Part Six Halloween Celebrations

and suggestions

Activities

Write a brief paragraph about your personal favorite memory that is associated with Halloween.

Begin by working in a group. imagine that you're participating in an event for

Halloween and require the "booth" to display your carnival merchandise. The group needs to come to the consensus of what they want to accomplish and then develop an inventory of what needed to realize their dream.

Create a costume for Halloween and include a list of all the items you'll require for your costume. Be aware that costumes for Halloween should not be scary. If you're looking for something more personal to dress up as the fictional character you think of as a hero, an famous person, or the god of your religion that you are awestruck by.

Do some independent research about one of the holiday dates that are similar to Halloween, like The Day of the Dead or The Festival of the Hungry Ghost. If you'd rather researching one of the festivals of the past that fall on Samhain as well as Pomona.

As a family or class make one of the classic Halloween desserts. These recipes of Soul

Cakes, Barmbrack, Candy Apples or Caramel Apples are all readily available. (Barmbrack and Soul Cake recipes can be found on the following webpage!). Be sure to ask an adult to supervise.

Make your own Jack O lantern face. You can sketch out the face and possibly color it, or even paint it onto the pumpkin. If all the safety precautions is in place, and supervision by an adult is in place, you could opt to carve pumpkins.

Discuss your personal fears with your family or friends. You could also study the most frequently feared fears are.

Classic Halloween Foods

Barmbrack:

2 1/2 Cups Chopped Dried Mixed Fruit

1 1/2 cups Hot Brewed Tea

2.25 Cups of Flour

1 Teaspoon Ground Cinnamon

12 Teaspoon of ground Nutmeg

12 Teaspoon of Baking Soda

1 Egg

1.1/2 Cups of Sugar

1/8 Cup of Lemon Marmalade

1 teaspoon of Grated Orange Zest (orange peel)

Directions:

1. Soak Dried Fruit in hot tea for two hours. Then drain and squeeze out the excess tea.

2. Pre-heat oven to 350 degrees F. Grease the bottom of a 9" Bundt pan.

3. Mix the flour, cinnamon, Nutmeg, and Baking Soda and set aside.

4. Beat the egg with sugar, marmalade, citrus zest and tea-soaked fruits until they are well blended. Blend into the flour until blended, and then pour into the bundt pan.

5. Bake in the oven for one hour, or until topping of cake is firm when lightly

pressing. Let it rest in pans for 2 hours before taking it out. Then, let it cool on the rack on a wire until at it is at room temperature.

(If you opt to include (if you choose to include "lucky objects" that are found in barmbrack, they can be inserted into the cake, or through the bottom, prior to serving).

Traditional Halloween Recipes

Soul Cakes:

1. Cup of Butter (2 sticks)

3 3/4 cups of Sifted Flour

1. Cup of Sugar

One Teaspoon (1/2 teaspoon) of Nutmeg

1 teaspoon of Cinnamon

1. Teaspoon of Ginger

1. Teaspoon of Allspice

2 Eggs

2 teaspoons Vinegar

4 - 6 Tablespoons Milk

Powdered Sugar

Directions:

1. Pre-heat oven until 350 degrees F.

2. Mix the butter and the flour with a large fork (or pastry blender)

3. Mix with sugar, ginger, nutmeg, cinnamon, and allspice.

4. Mix the egg, vinegar with milk.

5. Mix the flour and water mixture until a dough is formed.

6. Knead the dough thoroughly, and then roll it out until it's about 1/4 of an inch thick.

7. Make use of an oval 3" cookie cutter to cut the dough. Spread the dough out on a greased baking sheet and poke them many times with the fork.

8. Bake for 20 to 25 minutes.

9. Dust lightly with sugar powder when it is still warm.

Halloween Movie Suggestions (animated)

With Halloween coming up the perfect time to host a movie night and enjoy some of your family's most loved terrifying (or less frightening) films. If you're short of ideas, here are few ideas that you and your children might appreciate.

Remember that every child is different and each family has different standards of conduct. What is acceptable to the majority might not be appropriate to others. Always watch a preview of any film before watching with children.

The Great Pumpkin, Charlie Brown: The Peanut's Gang gets into the spirit of the season in this classic from 1966.

This fun special is about Linus Van Pelt , a renowned actor and the fervent belief in the Great Pumpkin. As Linus as well as Sally Brown spend the entire night waiting for the legendary being to appear, Charlie Brown and the gang get trick or treating and go to a Halloween celebration. As they travel, take a journey with Snoopy, the World War I Flying Ace (Snoopy) as he navigates through in the "French landscape". Your kids will be thrilled by this delightful story that has become a custom in the homes of many families.

Not Rated For All Audiences: Safe for all viewers

Run Time: 25 mins

Garfield's Halloween Adventure (aka Garfield in disguise) The lasagne-loving overweight cat gets introduced to delights that Halloween brings in this jolly and entertaining tale.

Garfield and his friend, Odie, have fun selecting costumes for Halloween, and then they head out to trick or treating. While on their trip they are told a ghoulish tale of pirates and hidden treasures. They even get chased by ghost pirates! The hilarious show was released in 1985, during the time that Garfield's popularity reached its highest.

Not Rated to be rated. Safe for all audiences.

Run Time: 25 mins

Monster House: Here's a visually captivating animation from the year 2006, which is just right for Halloween.

Two boys, DJ and Chowder, as they watch their cranky older neighbor Nebbercracker begin to suspect that their man's home is in fact a living monster. With the assistance of their new pal, Jenny Chowder, the two boys set out to discover the mystery. The film is voiced by the skills from Steve Buscemi, Maggie Gyllenhaal, Fred Willard, John Heder and many more.

Rated: PG with violent and scary images (fairly frightening for a PG-rated animated film)

Running Time in Time: 91 minutes

The Nightmare Before Christmas: This stop-motion animated movie from 1993 has such a distinctive style and look that it's bound to capture the imagination.

Jack Skellington, the King of Halloweentown is fed up by his life. When he takes a long stroll through the forest, he stumbles upon an opening that takes him to Christmasland. Jack is suddenly obsessed with the thought of Christmas. He along with fellow Halloweentown residents attempt to recreate the Christmas season with their own twist. The film was created by Tim Burton and features music and songs by Danny Elfman (who also provides the voice of Jack Skellington).

Rated as PG for some violent or scary images (however keep in mind that this is an animated movie and nothing is'realistic')

Run Time: 76 mins.

Halloween: Halloween Movie Suggestions (live-action)

As Halloween is near the perfect time to host a movie night and enjoy the family's most loved terrifying (or not too frightening) films. If you're looking for ideas, here are couple of suggestions you and your kids could like.

Remember that every child is unique and every family is governed by different standards for decency. What is acceptable to the majority might not be appropriate to others. Be sure to preview any film prior to watching with children.

The Private Eyes: Starring Don Knotts and Tim Conway,

Here's a movie that everyone will appreciate.

If Lord Morley is found dead Two investigators, Inspector Winship and Dr. Tart are called in to investigate the murder. They arrive at Morley Manor to discover that the house is full of strange characters, and possibly one or two ghosts! Begin with the hilarious pair as they try to solve the mystery in the hilarious comedy of 1980.

Rated by PG for some light violence, and a few scary images.

Running Length: 91 mins

Clue: Who is it? The Professor Plum sitting in the Conservatory with the candlestick?

This fun film was released in 1985 and is based on the well-known board game of the identical name. A group of six people get invited into a house, where they are required to cooperate in solving a murder. As the story unfolds, there are many unexpected twists and turns. Additionally The dvd (or Blue-Ray) version includes numerous endings, adding an element of surprise every watching. The film also boasts an impressive ensemble cast that include Tim Curry, Madeline Kahn, Martin Mull, Christopher Lloyd, Eileen Brennan and Michael McKean.

Rated: PG with light violence and mild language and jokes that are that may be considered adult-oriented.

Running Time: Time: 94 minutes

The Haunted Mansion: Here's a entertaining film for kids to like, based on the cult Disneyland attraction with the similar name.

The real estate professional (portrayed in the film by Eddie Murphy) and his family are visiting an old and decaying New Orleans mansion. In the wake of an unexpected heavy downpour, the family must spend the evening in the mansion. As night wears on, they discover that the home has been home to a variety of ghostly inhabitants, some of whom are unwilling to let their family leave. This film was made in 2003. film also features lots of fascinating effects and visuals that will keep children entertained.

Rated: PG with scary images, mild violence , and extremely mild language.

The Running Time is 99 mins

Tower of Terror: Based on an amusement park's most popular attraction, this made-for-TV film in 1997 is a fun adventure.

A lift falls 11 stories and leaves the hotel haunted by five ghosts. A half-century later a depressed journalist and his daughter attempt to solve the mystery. There's more than one unexpected twist in this story and children are bound to be entertained by the film. The film stars Steve Guttenberg and a young Kirsten Dunst.

Not Rated: Scary images that might irritate youngsters.

Running Time 90 minutes

Monster Squad Monster Squad: Developed in the style of the classic Universal "monster films" The film features all the iconic characters you'd imagine to find.

A group of youngsters who are obsessed by movies about monsters, create the club they refer to as "The Monster Squad". They don't realize that Dracula as well as Frankenstein's Monster as well as the Wolfman as well as The Mummy as well as Dracula and the Creature of The Black Lagoon have decided to visit their town. When the kids discover what's really going on, they seek to convince the adults about the truth and battle the monsters at one at the same time.

Rated as PG: contains violenceand violent or scary images. Also, there is vulgar language that is that is spoken by teenagers or preteens. (Should be kept for children older than).

Halloween: Safety Tips for Trick-or-Treat

Make sure you have the flashlight as well as wear something with reflective or wear something that shines.

It's better to start earlier than later. It's not necessary to delay Halloween trick-or-treating until later into the night. (6:00 pm to 9:00 pm is suggested).

Plan your routes ahead of time and know where you're going prior to when you take off.

Avoid costumes that slide across the ground. There are more injuries caused by falling over their costumes than any other thing during Halloween!

If wearing a mask make sure that the mask allows complete vision and breath. Be sure to look through your eye-holes, and that you breathe in a proper manner.

Be cautious when crossing streets or when you are in the driveways in front. Always keep an eye out for vehicles.

*Only go to trick-or-treat homes with a good amount of light (make sure that they have a porch light on) Be sure to be sure to stay in neighborhoods you are familiar with.

Don't eat the candy until you bring it home, and your parent or trusted adult has a look.

Make sure that you're with an adult and never trick or treat in groups.

Respect the property of others. Don't damage flower beds by tramples or damage their ornaments.

Chapter 5: The First Halloween

The story of the origins and development of Halloween can be traced back to thousands of years prior to the pagan, ancient Celtic New Year customs of "Samhain" which falls on the 1st of November. In the past, Celts lived in present-day Ireland, Scotland and Great Britain before Christianity was introduced to this region of the globe. Samhain is one of the pagan celebrations of religious significance which are linked to the passage of time which is in this case it was autumn paving the way for winter. Samhain signified the conclusion of the autumn harvest, the time that winter came to an end and the dark part of the year started. Samhain was a time of celebration for the Celts. Celts believed that on the night prior to Samhain on October 31 spirit of the deceased were allowed to come into the world of humans. In this was referred to as "All Hallow's Day" which is the Scottish Gaelic term - and is where the term Halloween originates.

Honoring the Dead

There are many cultures throughout the world that have different variations of this, for instance, The Day of the Dead in Mexico and The Festival of Lanterns in Japan. They all believe that the dead and loved ones are returned to the world of the living and that humans recognize their presence by honoring the spirits by offering them sweets and food. It was the same in the case of All Hallow's Eve. A time of magic in which spirits and humans (and fairy-worshippers!) were part of the same world and a one aspect of the pagan celebration involved laying out dishes of food that were offered to delight the spirits of the dead. Even if the food appeared as if it was not touched and was clean, people believed the Celts were of the belief it was believed it was believed the "essence" that the meal contained would be passed on to spirits. Families would often prepare a meal on their tables for relatives who had passed away.

Costumes and Trick-or Treating

On Samhain in the past, the ancient Celts used to make huge bonfires, and then dress themselves in headdresses and animal furs to protect themselves from evil spirits. These were the first costumes for Halloween! Later , Halloween customs to deter evil spirits included carving jack-o'-lanterns and dressing children (also called costume-making or"guising") to shield children from ghosts that could want to steal their human bodies! One of the reasons for "guising" kids was the need to conceal their identity in the dark when they went from door-to-door asking for food or money. This was the start of "trick-or-treating" however it didn't begin so sly or fun as you might imagine. Irish as well as Scottish children were required to pull a trick in order to entertain the members of the household prior to receiving their reward of a penny or piece of candy, or cake. This was usually done by singing a tune or writing the words of a poem (much as the Christmas carol). But the pagans also believe that the mischievous "little people" of their form as fairies or elves - were the reason for making it difficult during All Hallow's Eve.

Jack-o-Lanterns

Did you realize that the first jack-o'-lanterns were not even pumpkins? They aren't natives to Europe they were only popularized after Halloween was introduced to America. The first jack-o'-lanterns were constructed from beets, potatoes or turnips! The name "jack-o-lantern" comes because of an Irish story of an individual named "Stingy Jack." The legend goes the story goes that Stingy Jack was the first to convince the Devil to purchase drinks, and then got the money back away from the Devil. Over the course of time, Jack continued to trick the Devil and promised that if Jack passed away the Devil would not send him to the grave. God did not wish to see Stingy Jack in heaven too so the Devil sent him away to spend the night in the earth, with just a coal shard in hollow turnips to illuminate his path. The story is as follows and how a legend came to be the symbol of jack-o'lanterns. The people did not want Jack or other spirits of evil appearing at their houses during All Hallow's Eve, so they made the root vegetables, such as turnips, with scary faces and put the pumpkins on their doorsteps to scare them away.

Roman & Christian Influence

A few more symbols of what we have come to know in our modern-day Halloween customs developed when Christianity spread across Great Britain and Ireland almost two thousand years ago. It is believed that the Romans that conquered the areas took with them

Christian beliefs as well as their own mythology. Other Halloween rituals that probably be familiar to you, like bobbing for apples or drinking apple cider originate out of the Roman tradition of earlier festival known as"the "Feast of Pomona" (named in honor of the Roman goddess of orchards). It is important to remember that it was during this time period that the majority of cultures celebrated natural-based celebrations around the changing of the seasons , often with old-fashioned beliefs and customs that were tied to various Gods as well as Goddesses. At the autumn harvest's end was the abundance of apples, making it an ideal time to make cider from apples - that was a perfect fit with pagan Celtic celebrations to mark the end season. The ancient tradition of bobbing apples was usually accompanied by a small coin hidden in the apple and people were not afraid of getting their heads immersed in water (they only had to be cautious to eat the apple from the case they bought one filled with coins!).

Like the Easter celebration (another old pagan celebration) The Roman Catholic Church incorporated new Christian holidays that were synchronized with old Celtic celebrations. In the year 850 The Catholic church changed its date for "All Saints Day" to the 1st of November as well as "All Soul's Day" on the 2nd of November - the fusion of pagan as well as Christian festivals and celebrations the reason behind why the customs of Halloween continue to thrive through the years. Also, when Christianity began to take over the role of the pagan faiths old Celtic rituals and rites that celebrated the various Gods were decried. They also demanded that the Catholic Church wanted all these ancient societies to switch to Christianity and to abandon their pagan practices and religions. That's where witches wearing black pointed hats, riding on broomsticks as well as the myths about black cats are a part of. The Halloween symbols were created over the years of Catholic Church in which non-

Christians and pagans to the Devil. Particularly during Medieval times, women (and men however, in smaller numbers) continued to heal people with herbs, just as they have been doing since the beginning of time. Imagine visiting your doctor's office and being told that the majority of people didn't have access to medical treatment or medicine. Instead , they relied on traditional formulas for healing (or you could refer to them as "potions") that were made of plants. Consider the familiar picture of the witch sitting over stirring a hot cauldron it is possible that she been the town's sole "doctor." It's enough to that this wasn't the best time to be conventional healers from Catholic Europe. This witch's image as well as the horror of being a witch, came to America together when the first Europeans who came to America during the 15th century and the image of the witch who was wicked is a constant part of our society ever since.

Halloween comes to America

In the early 1800's, nearly one million Irish immigrants came to America. U.S. due to the Great Potato Famine that decimated the primary crop that Irish people required to live. This number of Irish immigrants came roots in pagan and Catholic practices, which made Halloween in America an extremely popular and revived celebration. Halloween decorations were now made of huge orange pumpkins picked in autumn, and there were still bonfires of huge size that were lit and costumes worn for the celebration of October 31st. Although it had pagan Celtic origins, American Halloween traditions became focussed around fun costume, sweets and fun activities as of the time of the early 1900's. Families and parents didn't want their children to be terrified by scary things like Halloween witches or ghosts. The candy corn we know and love was invented around the 1880's specifically for Halloween. It was known as "chicken feed." The 1920's-1930's the candy industry realized that Halloween was now the most popular holiday in the United States and began advertising for trick-or-treaters. (Yes there were parents absconding with their children's Reese's peanut-butter cups 100 years ago!) There was no need for children to perform a song or dance to get their treats. They just needed to dress as their favorite characters and knock on doors to shout "TRICK or TREAT"! The idea of a "trick" isn't meant to be a real thing however it is one of the many traditions that have been observed during Halloween through the years.

Modern Halloween and Charities

As the fall season approaches families begin to get excited about choosing pumpkins to carve, and heading to the most popular attractions, such as corn mazes and hayrides , wagons, apple cider fresh from the trees and even CANDY! People who like the thrill of getting scared are able to find haunted homes in every town in the United States.

We love decorating our backyards with creepy skeletons, small homemade ghosts hanging from the trees while getting ourselves ready for Halloween trick-or-treaters. A lot of communities host "trunk-or-treat" events which allow families to take their kids to a local parking lot instead of going from door to door. Many churches open their doors for candy distribution to the children of the neighborhood dressed in costumes. There are a few, but not all people still give candy to trick-or-treaters. The most popular fundraisers are for charitable causes, such as Unicef which provides children with boxes that solicit donations for other children in need around the world. Many haunted homes are managed by local fire or police departments to provide a safe environment where children can enjoy an enjoyable spook-tacular night and raise money for community-based programs.

Modern Samhain Traditions

The meaning of jack-o'lanterns as well as witches, ghosts, bobbing for apples and treating-or-treating all go back to the earliest All Hallow's Eve traditions of the ancient festivals that marked the end of harvest. The modern-day the pagan faiths (Wiccans, Druids, and many more) all over the world observe Samhain as a sacred day that marks the end of the seasons and also the start in the pagan New Year. Many ways the modern-day practitioners of the "old methods" celebrate the conclusion of autumn's harvest, and the start of winter, and to remember the memory of their loved ones who passed away. Small altars are set up inside their homes, using natural items and the colours of the season that have been used in the past by the time of the ancient Celts. The traditional colors for Samhain are black and orange Are you familiar with them? Other symbols of the season include gourds, pumpkins, cornstalks, and apples. Many pagans build altars for their ancestral homes with images or other mementos from relatives and friends who died and use small candles to commemorate their memory, similar to other festivals mentioned previously that include that is, Mexican Day of the Dead as well as The Japanese Festival of Lanterns. Some still follow the tradition of holding the traditional "Feast to commemorate the dead" and setting a table of food to the spirits of the deceased, and many modern pagans use to observe this holiday as an intimate way to connect with the season by walking in nature , or reflecting on the year that has passed and what they anticipate for the coming year. A popular custom during Samhain is to note down any events on tiny pieces of paper that are negative or require to be released (emotionally) prior to the beginning of the start of the new year. They then burn them in a fire . This is called the "letting let go" ceremony. You don't need to be a pagan in order to perform any of these rituals however, you do not have to prepare a spot on the table for your loved ones who have passed away as well! It's simply necessary to recognize that many of these ancient Celtic customs are still followed by a large number of people across the world who consider Samhain as well as All Hallow's Eve as a holy religious holiday.

Halloween Decor & Crafts

There are a myriad of ways we can (and most likely have already done without even realizing it) incorporate small pieces of fall decorations to our yards and homes to be in the spirit of Halloween. Pumpkins and jack-o-lanterns are of course, an obvious choice however what about DIY wreaths made of tiny, vibrant dried corn and acorns or scarecrows that are stuffed with straw, fashioned from old clothes placed on a bale hay? These are all festive decorations that are a result of celebrating the close of the harvest! Do you want your decorations to be more spooky yet still enjoyable for children? A simple craft that children of all ages will delight in is creating tiny ghosts that you can hang from the branches of trees or on the eaves of your home's front. You can buy tennis balls or similar size Styrofoam globes from your local craft store, then cut small pieces of white fabric (you might even make use of an old piece of cloth) which you put around your balls using an elastic band. Be sure you leave enough fabric to hang it down and blow up in the breeze. Make faces for ghosts - scary or humorous hanging them on strings or fishing lines that are clear. Children who aren't old enough to make their own pumpkins are able to make faces on their own miniature pumpkins to help decorate. Another great Halloween activity for kids is making an edible Candy corn-themed wreath (especially when they can consume portions of "supplies "!). The only thing you have to do is purchase the Styrofoam wreath or sturdy circle at the local craft store and after which you can paint the wreath black, and let your children make use of craft glue to fill the wreath with pieces of candy corn. You could even make an orange or black bow on the wreath after the glue has dried and the wreath is more festive.

Halloween Party Food & Games

Planning a Halloween or party themed birthday celebration at home? The possibilities are endless when it comes to Halloween-themed desserts. Don't forget to add Apple cider, the caramel apples and roasting pumpkin seeds! Roasting the seeds of your pumpkin jack-o'-lantern is easyto do: clean and dry out the pumpkin's seeds using couple of newspaper towels (make sure there aren't strings of pumpkin pulp hanging) and then heat oven to 300°F (150 degrees Celsius) and then toss them in bowls and cover with melting butter and salt prior to placing them on a cookie tray and baking between 40 and 45 minutes. Cupcakes made of pumpkin with cream cheese frosting can be a wonderful alternative to a normal birthday cake or for a treat. Instead of regular platters of fruit or vegetables set out "ghost" bananas (peeled bananas cut in half, and three chocolate chips to make the mouth and eyes) as well as miniature "pumpkins" (peeled tangerines that have small "stalk" with celery in the middle). Make everyone squirm a bit by serving devilled eggs with black olives in the shape of huge black spiders. One of the most popular games for any event, or trick-or-treaters is to blindfold the eggs and then have them put their hands into bowls of freshly cut and peeled grape "eyeballs" along with prepared spaghetti "brains." If you're truly motivated to make a more lively game, make use of (or ask someone else to help you use) an jigsaw for cutting out the face and shape of a massive jack-o'lantern paint it, and then make it an especially fun beanbag toss. If that's not possible it's also possible to use an enormous piece of strong cardboard to create the jack-o'lantern toss bean bag and then place wood pieces behind it to give it additional support. Make the most of Halloween-themed decorations, sweets and other toys to make gift bags for guests celebrating birthdays.

Trick-or-treating can be fun enough What makes modern-day Halloween as thrilling? COSTUMES! It's the only night of the year when we can dress and "guise" as anyone or whatever we choose to be. You can alter your appearance by dressing as any character from our fantasy world we want to. There's something quite relaxing (maybe even fantastical) about being able take our fears off and be completely free to create a new persona, from the sweetest fairy tale princesses to the most disgusting or creepy monsters. No matter who we decide to take on the process of planning costumes is a major aspect of our contemporary All Hallow's Eve celebration. Get out there and pick the best costume and carving pumpkins this year!

Halloween began with the old Celts

"Samhain," the word "Samhain" is "summer's conclusion" in Gaelic which is the language spoken among the Celts.

As you may have guessed, Samhain took place at the season's end that is also the time of the closing of the harvest season.

The time of harvesting at the end of the year is the perfect time to gather the harvest and store the rest for the winter months.

In the month of Samhain this time of year, Celtic people rejoiced in the change of the seasons as well as the food they grew in the previous year.

They had huge bonfires and even wore costumes as the ones we wear today.

What kind of costumesare you wearing?

They donned all sorts of costumes.

However, the costumes they favored to wear most...

Animal skins and head of animals (from authentic animals)!

In the year 43 the Romans took over the Celtic area.

The Romans were known for their own festivals similar to Samhain.

They also incorporated the Roman festival with Samhain.

The Romans played a role in the development of Halloween.

The most famous of Roman celebrations was Feralia which was a day that fell in late October. the Romans commemorated those who had died.

Another day of celebration was to celebrate Pomona Pomona, one of the Roman goddess of trees and fruits.

The emblematic of Pomona is the apple.

Have you ever played with apples during Halloween?

You then took part in a Halloween celebration that could go all the way to Pomona.

The practice of bobbing apples dates back many years.

A few years later, the Pope began a celebration to pay tribute to saints and people who died.

It was also known as All Souls Day.

The festival spread across the Celtic regions and was merged together with Samhain along with the Roman festival.

All Souls Day was celebrated by big bonfires, parades and costumes.

All Souls Day was also known as All Saints Day, All Hallows Eve and All Hallowmas?

Are you beginning to feel familiar?

This is right, All Hallows Eve and All Hallowmas eventually became Halloween!

One thing the Irish used to do was to cut turnips and place small candles or coals inside.

They took them out of their residences during All Hallows Eve to keep the evil spirits out.

When the Irish made their way to America they noticed that there was a large amount of pumpkins.

They were also more straightforward to carve than turnips.

They began carving pumpkins, and placing candles inside.

This is how Jack-o-Lanterns started!

The Middle Ages took place about 1,000 years ago.

In that period, the people living in poverty living in Ireland or Britain would be "souling."

This would mean they'd go knocking on doors All Hallowmas.

As soon as the door was is opened they will offer prayers for the deceased relatives of the persons who resided in the home.

In return, the house owners would present them with the home owners a Soul Cake.

What? !

Soul Cake was a Soul Cake was a small round cake.

After you had eaten Soul Cake Soul Cake, a dead soul's soul was taken to heaven.

This is how trick-or-treating started.

Nowadays, people carve a lots of pumpkins, and eat plenty of sweets.

About 1.1 million pounds of pumpkins is grown throughout the United States each year.

And what about candy?

Over $2 billion worth of sweets is sold every annually in America.

Candy bars made of chocolate are the most loved Halloween sweet.

Candy corn aren't going away. They're in the top ten most-sold Halloween candy items.

What kind of costumes do people prefer to dress up for Halloween?

Many different things.

The most requested costumes for children include:

Princess

Witch

Spiderman

Pirate

Pumpkin

Vampire

Disney Princess

Star Wars Character

Tinker Bell

Batman

What do you want to have for this Halloween?

Why do we have so many witches on Halloween?

The roots of this all go back to the early Celts.

It was believed that when someone passed away, their soul would go to a cauldron of witches.

A cauldron is a large pot for cooking on an open flame.

The souls once were in the cauldron...

A witch stirred the pot to allow souls to return to the world of.

Have you ever seen a bat at Halloween?

In the past there was a belief that when you observed a bat flying around your home three times, someone was bound to be killed!

If the bat flew into your home during the night of Halloween...

Then your home was the site of a haunting!

But that's not all.

If a spider gets caught in an open lamp that is lit by candles and the flame burns...

There is a witch in the area!

Have you ever witnessed a large pumpkin?

Do you mean really large?

If you've had one you have a pumpkin, I'm betting it was not as large as a pumpkin was growing in Canada.

This is because that pumpkin weighed a staggering 1,446 pounds!

In October 2004, the huge pumpkin was proclaimed to be the largest pumpkin ever in the world during the annual pumpkin festival located in Port Elgin, Ontario, Canada.

The night before Halloween is believed that spirits of evil lurk at every turn.

It's an excellent idea that you keep your children as far from you as you can.

Do you want to know the most effective ways to dissuade an evil spirit?

Ring an alarm!

This is what they say.

I'm thinking of trying it to ensure my safety!

Be on the lookout for Halloween.

There is no way to know for sure what may witness.

Or who's looking at you!

Here's what I am referring to...

You might be out trick-or treating.

Everything is going well.

Everyone is awestruck by your costume, and you'll be able to get lots of candy.

Then...

You meet the web of a spider.

It's just a squirt, you think?

Perhaps it is an angelic spirit from a deceased loved one watching you?

They say that!

Do you want meeting a witch Halloween night?

I would not.

Yet... for the case that you'd like to... Here's the procedure:

Your clothes are put inside out.

It's not the most bizarre part.

Then return to the beginning.

Then...

You might even be lucky enough to meet an occult.

This is what they say!

This is a last trick to make your Halloween really memorable.

Let's say that you've carved out 27 large pumpkins.

They look amazing.

I'm talking about really cool.

It's impossible to wait for your friends to meet them.

And, one week before the Halloween celebration...

You head out to look over your work and only discover...

Your pumpkins are shriveled!

Similar to raisins.

This is bad news.

What can you do now?

Do you spend all day and at night, sculpting new ones?

Shut the doors, switch off your lights and wait for your guests don't visit your home?

Imagine you're sick, so you have a reason not to celebrate Halloween?

No Yes, No and NO!

The answer is straightforward.

Simply fill the tub with water.

The pumpkins should be placed in the pots.

Soak them overnight then...

PRESTO!

In the next morning, they'll return in their round smiley forms.

October 30th - The most terrifying evening of the season!

Every year, on this evening, people gather to celebrate Halloween. There are many traditions associated with the holiday that aren't known to the majority of people. A very popular custom you may see are people dressed in costumes for Halloween, many of which depict terrifying monsters and dead in the tradition of the festival. Everything else, from superheroes to peanut butter and jelly is equally fair.

Halloween was actually the holiday which marked the end of harvest and the beginning of winter. It was considered to be an event that featured super-ordinary creatures and characters from the Deceased were seen roaming the planet. The lanterns were used during the when they were used to depict the supernatural creatures who were said to be in the nighttime during Halloween. In addition, they were employed as a defense mechanism to make the spirits feel uncomfortable.

Kids are the most likely to be walking around dressed in these clothes, sounding doorbells and yelling trick-or-treat with the hopes of securing candy bars and other treats.

Houses are often decorated to look like an unsettling location (of-course with a lighter aspect) and parties are celebrated in cinemas that are frightening by sculpting faces into them and candle light fixtures placed inside pumpkins to be displayed on screens.

Hayrides, corn puzzles, terrifying stories, bizarre music, haunted houses, pumpkin cakes, apple cider and all of these make the evening an enjoyable experience. But, imagine the event to someone who was not anticipating the event.

It's amazing how strange everything seems to the people. It is important to ask what the reason behind these actions what is the reason, and where did this season of Christmas originate and how far it is.

We guarantee you that you have no idea about the history that shaped the origins of Halloween.

SAMHAIN TWISTED INTO THE HALLOWEEN

Halloween is a holiday of patchwork which ties together rituals of society.

The whole thing started with the Celts who had spread throughout Europe more than two thousand years prior. October 31st was the date when they enjoyed themselves after the harvesting time in the celebration known as SAMHAIN. This evening also signified that it was the Celtic New Year and considered as a magical time in which the souls of the dead entered the earth. This was the time that they were encased in a cloak of death and life was thought to be at its smallest during Samhain.

The villager gathered and lit massive bonfires to bring the dead back to the spirit realm and to keep them away from the grave.

At night, before SAMHAIN the people held believed that the dead returned as ghosts. They would keep food and red wine in their front doors to provide them with food and also wear ghost masks that could be misinterpreted by other demons.

Christian churches were renamed SAMHAIN to All Saints Day or All Hallows day in the eighth century. The night prior to it was actually All Hallows' Eve, which later changed to Halloween!

The STORY OF WITCHES

Witches are a popular Halloween character who are usually dressed in black, with a green body with a sharp cap soaring the broom throughout at Full Moon.

They're not just an item for Halloween, however they have a story that we did not know. The story of witches comes from the traditional western cultures and people believed that witches were responsible for accidents, storms as well as other negative issues and are seen as symbols of bad energy. While it's an illusion people used to think about Witches as being the spirits that were accountable for all negative energy.

Witch Hat:

The members of Europe of the elite divisions wore similar dark, high pointed hats during the 15th century. This is why the image of Witch Hat was removed out of them.

Brooms:

Common household tools used to meet crops and for imagination. it's believed that witches make use of Brooms to hide their wands and use them to perform black magic.

TRICK OR TREAT HISTORIZATION - From GUISING AND SOULING

SOUL

In the Older times, during the course of All Souls day which was celebrated on the 2nd on November 2, Needy could beg Pastries known as soul cakes''. In the return, they were asked to be a blessing to the dearly deceased.

GUIDING

Teenagers would dress up in fancy attire and would accept contributions including cash, food items and other donations to perform Pranks, signing events, and various other activities that are fun for the kids.

The 19th century was the time when Irish and Scottish immigrants in the 19th century. The United States introduced these customs , which are now referred to as TRICK or TREATING.

The customs were reformed in 1950. This led to the current children's friendly cantered celebration making it the second highest commercially-driven holiday, after Christmas.

HISTORY of PUMPKINS in the HALLOWEEN

I'm sure that a number of you have made an ominous face into a pumpkin, and displayed it on your front porch or on your balcony during the time of Halloween. Pumpkins are the norm for Halloween, and possibly a signal for the most terrifying evening of the year. But, have you ever thought prior to carving a pumpkin if it's an odd choice? If we look the development of the method back, we can observe exactly the way this particular method came into existence and how it progressed to the point it is at current.

The pumpkin figurine is really more than you think. To learn more details about it, we'll explore JACK O LANTERN.

JACK O LANTERN AND PUMPKINS

We all know that the jack-o'-lantern as one of the most well-known symbols of Halloween. But, where exactly did this tradition come from? What's the story that lies the reason behind this practice of carving the jack-o'lantern?

Let's find out how it was born from Irish myths.

In an ancient Irish legend, there was a person known as the stingy Jack. He was a snobby old man who loved making fun of everyone including his friends and family members and even the Devil himself.

A few nights ago the stingy Jack was able to invite the devil to share an alcoholic drink with him. Being stingy, he refused to purchase the beverage instead, he convinced the devil to turn it into a coin that could later be used to purchase the drink. Instead of spending the money on the drinks, Jack chose to keep the coin and allowed the devil back to his normal style in the hope that he not bother Jack for a whole year.

A year later, Jack fooled the devil into climbing the tree. Jack did not want to help him down , unless he pledged not to bother him for the next ten years.

In exchange for this deal, the devil also agreed to not reveal Jack's soul after Jack dies. Jack passed away, but God could not let the entry of such a person into heaven and the devil remained true in his word and refused to let Jack into his realm. Devil truly felt compassion for the man and handed him a charcoal piece so to allow him to see into the darkness and be destined to wander the earth for the rest of his life.

Jack used a turnip to hold the charcoal he was burning in order to ignite his path. A lot of Irish people reported that they had observed this supernatural figure , which they started calling Jack from the Lantern. In the end, the name was changed to Jack-o'-lantern.

It became a common practice in Ireland to make jack-o'lanterns out of hollowed-out turnipsand beets and potatoes. However the time that Irish immigrants moved to America in the late 1800s, they discovered a new vegetable that went perfectly with the purpose better. The pumpkins that were native to The Northern America and

Canada were found to be excellent for carving and creating the popular jack-o'-lanterns we know and celebrated today, making Halloween the second biggest holiday across America. U.S.A. after Christmas.

Chapter 6: A Brief Origins Of Halloween

Halloween's roots, like the majority of other modern European celebrations, could be traced to the time before Christianity. In the early days, the Celtic peoples were settled by numerous tribes that are today France, Ireland, and Great Britain. The early Celts were a distinct people with the Celtic language of their own, beliefs of pagan origins and calendars, which split the year in two halves that was winter and summer. The dark time of the season, winter where agriculture was not possible started in November with October 31, the day that marked the end day of the previous year. Similar to that, it was the day that harvest was finished.

It was a time of celebration. New Year and the completion of fieldwork took a full week. The first night of November fell during mid-season of festival. Samhain is "the closing of the summer" on the local dialect was the name given today from the Celts. Alongside the distribution of the harvest on this day, it was customary to celebrate the deceased. There was a belief that during the night between the end of the year and the first date of each year there was a entrance to the tomb was opened.

the other side of the world opens and the souls of the deceased ghosts and spirits, appear to the world.

To ensure that they did not become a casual victim of the creatures of the afterlife In order to avoid being a victim of the afterlife, the Celts were dressed as animals and quit their dark homes in the evening, where delicious offerings were made to ghosts. They then gathered around enormous, two-row flames, that were bred by Druids. Between the two fires they would walk through the entire tribe holding children and leap onto smaller burning fires. The fire's force was believed to cleanse people and allow them enter New Year's Eve New Year with a pure soul. In the celebration, a part of the animals were cut off, and the carcasses of animals killed were placed in the Sacred Fire, and the future was predicted based on the drawings made by the burning bones.

In addition there is a tradition to create vegetable faces to express different emotions.

The carving was performed on turnips, which is a kind of fodder turnedip used to feed livestock. Everybody carried an empty "head" made of turnips when they left the main evening celebration of Samhain celebration. Inside of which were put hot coals that were a part of the Sacred Fire. In the early morning the lamp was lit, it prevented evil spirits from roaming the streets. The man who developed the concept to create Jack Lamp. Jack Lamp.

The ancient customs of celebrations for New Year's Eve and the Celtic New Year were passed through generations up to the point of the modern era.

Following the conquest of the Romans and the Romans, the Celts changed their religion into Christianity and were made to give up their pagan practices. However, with the rise of Catholicism and the advent of Catholicism, Samhain was suddenly given an overhaul and the old Celtic customs of the celebration were preserved in the Catholic celebration that was All Saints' Day that was observed on November 1. The holiday is known as Hallows-Even in English the Hallowes Evan holiday or "Evening of Saints" and eventually gained an abbreviated form that was incorporated into the contemporary holiday of halloween (Halloween). The same time Halloween gained a dark reputation as a pagan black celebration during time of the Middle Ages, when it was described in the same manner from Christian monks.

Holiday symbols

The night prior to the celebration All Saints Day is observed in accordance with changing times, however, it is still held to the core characteristics, Celtic beliefs. On Halloween, people dress up in carnival costumes as well as organize celebrations and parties. The most prominent symbol of the day is a lantern made from an enormous pumpkin. The Celts made these lamps to mark the harvest and to help those who have died discover their way towards the opposite side of the world with a lamp. The original vegetable was used to feed turnips, but with the arrival of Thanksgiving to America, the United States, pumpkin became more well-known as a food that was more widespread and less expensive during the fall season.

The most well-known Halloween costumes are monsters, vampires, werewolves as well as witches, ghosts and many other mythical heroes that are usually deemed scary.

Celebrities decorate their homes with the theme of fall, pumpkin lamps are hung on the porch or window sills. In addition to the vegetable lanterns, the most popular objects for decoration include garden scarecrows made of paper, wooden skeletons made of plastic, spiders candles, and compositions made from dry leaves and plants. According to tradition, the primary colours of the holiday were shades of black and orange.

Lamp Jack

The large, ripe pumpkin with a terrifying face that is lit with a candlelight inside, was the principal image of the Halloween celebration. The lantern made from a homemade recipe earned the name of the Jack's Lamp, or Jack's Lantern. The story of the creation of this striking image of Christmas is entwined with an old Irish legend.

The legend goes it is believed that Jack was an ironsmith who was extremely shrewd and hungry to drink and spend money. The residents of his community get so sick of his irritating drinking partner that there's just no reason to not have a drink with the man. Then Jack suggested that Lucifer and him have one bottle of wine at the nearby restaurant. Lucifer was willing to be with him. Then, when it was time to purchase the beverage, Jack offered the naive Satan to transform into a coin to which he also accepted. The clever blacksmith, not ever thinking twice, immediately put it in his pocket which was already waiting for a cross that was already prepared.

Lucifer was caught in a trap that he was in unable escape from the trap that included images of Jesus Christ as the Savior. Jack fell under Satan's influence and accepted to be released as a condition of a pledge to help the blacksmith in whatever way that he could.

Conclusion

I hope you've gained an understanding of the origins of Halloween, and how we continue to celebrate it this year. Now is the time to to select the pumpkins you'll need to carve and costumes for the night! Have fun decorating your home and eating all the delicious treats and are sure to have a wonderful Halloween!

www.ingramcontent.com/pod-product-compliance
Lightning Source LLC
Chambersburg PA
CBHW060329030426
42336CB00011B/1256